BAY CITY BABYLON

The **Unbelievable** but True Story of the **Bay City Rollers**

(An unauthorized biography)

Wayne Coy

Cactus Moon Publishing

Bay City Babylon:
The Unbelievable But True Story of the Bay City Rollers

Published by Hats Off Books™
610 East Delano Street, Suite 104, Tucson, Arizona 85705 U.S.A.
www.hatsoffbooks.com

LCCN 2005922358
ISBN 1587364638

For Kris, Ian, Gavin, Savannah, and Cameron Coy. It's done. And I love you for putting up with me.

TABLE OF CONTENTS

The Real Thing

Screw the critics and the naysayers, if the Ramones thought you were cool then that's a lofty badge of honor you can proudly wear forever.

Johnny, Joey, Dee Dee, and Tommy Ramone loved the Bay City Rollers. They saw through the massive hype and the unyielding critical backlash. They simply "got" it. In fact, they loved the bubblegum sensibility of the band so much that they borrowed the mighty celebratory chant of the group's biggest U.S. smash, "Saturday Night" and cleverly reconfigured it (replacing the S-A-T-U-R-D-A-Y Night! with "Hey Ho Let's Go!") into their own meteoric punk rock anthem, "Blitzkrieg Bop."

Plain and simple, the Bay City Rollers are one of the '70s most criminally underrated pop acts. Throughout the Super Seventies, from "Bye Bye Baby" to "Saturday Night," "Yesterday's Hero," to "I Only Wanna Be With You," the Bay City Rollers delivered some of the most deliciously commercial pop of its time. A global phenomenon that brought to mind Beatlemania circa 1964, the Bay City Rollers captured the world with timeless melodically sublime anthems that deeply resonated with their huge and loyal fanbase.

Breaking free from the shackles of their management, narrow minded record company, and to some extent their dyed in the wool fans, The BCR's transformation into The Rollers on the *Elevator* album is arguably their crowning moment as a band. A marvelous power pop triumph, *Elevator* brilliantly demonstrates that these weren't bubble-headed pop pretenders, but the real thing. The addition of multi-talented singer/songwriter Duncan Faure made all the difference. The album reaped major critical praise (a first for them) and truly showed off a band dying to reveal their true selves to the world.

Above all, The Bay City Rollers celebrated fun and good times. And in today's troubled climate that's a great lesson to impart to the world. So break out the tartan and wear it proudly, Wayne Coy's *Bay City Babylon* provides a compelling tale of Scotland's finest musical export. I hope you enjoy reading it as much as I did.

—Ken Sharp

Ken Sharp is the author/co-author of seven music books including tomes on Raspberries, The Beatles, Cheap Trick, Eric Carmen, KISS, Power Pop music and Small Faces.

PROLOGUE

The O.B.B.

It's an interesting reaction. The one you get in America when telling people that you are writing a book about the Bay City Rollers. If it's in person, it's a vacant look followed by a puzzled expression and then "uh, what songs do they sing?" or, "is that a football team?" If it's on the phone, I enjoy the pregnant pause and then imagine the person on the other end of the line with a vacant look and puzzled expression. Inevitably, I say, "You know, 'S-A-T-U-R-D-A-Y Night,'" and they say "Ooooh! The Bay City Rollers." That process is known in the research business as "aided recall." Yeah, *very* aided.

So, the question does bear asking: Why a book about the Bay City Rollers?

Well for starters, they sold over one hundred million records in a very short period of time (1971 to '79). They elicited a reaction from—and made an impact on—a young audience unlike any pop group since the Beatles. Say what you will about the redemptive qualities of the music; the mania was one hundred percent real and way beyond the adulation brought on by other post-Fab Four phenomena, including the Monkees, David Cassidy, and the Osmonds. It was a brief but oh-so-strong "teen-quake" felt all over the world. Bedroom walls of teen and pre-teen girls from Bangkok to Belfast to Brussels to Berkeley featured the smiling faces of the spiky haired Scots. They were truly a worldwide phenomenon.

Second, the Bay City Rollers saga is like a VH1 "Behind the Music" episode on steroids. You name it, it happened to these guys, and somehow, at the end of the day, they're all still standing. Barely. Some say a record company, merchandisers, and a calculating manager ripped them off in grandiose fashion. Others contend that they were victims of the simple naiveté that comes with venturing into uncharted business territory. They are musically maligned by some, while others call them the most underrated pop/rock group ever. Theirs is a story that has never been told objectively or completely. Until now.

Before there was Duran Duran or New Kids on the Block, before N-Sync or Backstreet Boys, there was the original boy band. The O.B.B. And this is their story…

ONE

Hey, Mister! Make Us Famous

When it came to pop music culture, Edinburgh, Scotland, in 1965 was not much different from the rest of the U.K. in that the Beatles and the Rolling Stones had blazed a trail—and that trail was there to run down for any British kids with guitars and a PA system. The one thing that separated Edinburgh from its neighbors in Ireland, Wales, England, and even Glasgow was that no one had successfully navigated that trail yet. But it wasn't for a lack of effort on the part of the kids. The youth clubs of Edinburgh were filled with aspiring Lennons and Jaggers all clumsily working on chords while affecting the look of their pop music heroes. Each one taking Dusty Springfield's advice, "Wishin' and Hopin'" that the hours of rehearsal would pay off in local notoriety—and maybe more. London was swinging, and Edinburgh's would-be rock stars were all dreaming of being there for the ride.

Seventeen-year-old Alan George Longmuir was one of those dreamers. "I remember seeing the Beatles on *Thank Your Lucky Stars* and *Ready Steady Go*, and that was it. I had to have a guitar just like everybody else that was into rock and roll at school." His cousin, Neil Porteous, beat Longmuir to the instrument du jour. Longmuir recalls, "Neil had his first and wanted someone to knock about with. I got a couple of jobs delivering milk, rolls in

11

the morning, and papers in the afternoon after school. I saved that money and bought a second-hand Spanish acoustic." Right behind him came his younger brother, Derek Macintosh Longmuir.

The rock and roll bug had also bitten the fair-haired four-teen-year-old, who'd gotten his first musical experience in the Boy's Brigade. "I was interested in drums and [wanted to] learn all about them. Although that was military-style drumming, not any pop stuff. We used to play on a wooden table. There might be eight guys around the table, plus the leader at the top. He took us through rudimentary things. You start with 'Scotland the Brave.' You just rat-tat-tat away at the table with your sticks until you're actually good enough to go on parade with a real drum." The real drums had to wait a while. The Ambassadors were formed with the younger Longmuir pounding out the rhythm on biscuit tins. Not so sexy, but functional. The "band" made their debut at a family wedding playing one number, the Everly Brothers' "Wake Up Little Susie." From that point on, it was off to the rock and roll races for Alan and Derek.

The Longmuir family was typical working-class Edinburgh. Father Duncan was an undertaker, and Mother Georgina was a homemaker taking care of the brood, which included Alan (b. 6/20/48) and Derek (b. 3/19/53) plus two Longmuir girls, Betty and Alice. Like so many up and down the block, the family's living-room furniture soon gave way to guitars, amps, and drums. Every day after school, the fledgling rockers would gather to carefully work on their repertoire, which consisted of mainly Motown and Beatles covers.

Tynecastle Secondary School was where Gordon "Nobby" Clark befriended Derek Longmuir. Clark was a member of the school choir and remembers discovering that his mate Derek had similar musical interests. "I had no idea they had a band. I just remembered Derek tapping away at the desk with his pencil in science class. That's how I first became aware that he was a drummer." Needing a singer, Clark was quickly enlisted by the group, who were now getting serious. Porteous scrapped his acoustic after getting an electric guitar for his birthday, which inspired Alan Longmuir to also go electric and switch to bass like fellow lefty Paul McCartney.

"I used to go to this guy Scott Murray's house. He was a bass player, and I would just watch him and figured that was the way to go. My first bass was an Egmund, made by Rosetti. One of the worst basses you could get, but it was all I could afford. I think it was around £33, which I actually paid up in installments."

It wasn't long before Duncan Longmuir succumbed to the pressure being applied by his youngest son and shelled out £60 for Derek's first drum kit. The practices continued in the front room and the band, now known as the Saxons, took out an ad in the paper for a rhythm guitarist. Alan remembers, "We got all sorts of guys coming up. Some were experienced; some were too old or bald. We were just starting out and wanted someone the same as us. Then, this guy Dave Pettigrew turned up. He was still in school and was quite good. He played 'Help' by the Beatles, and I was knocked out. I said, 'You're in.'" He was, and the band was set to make their first public appearance at Cairns Church Club. "It was our first real job in front of an audience," says Alan. "I was really nervous. We were not too sure of ourselves, but it was good because all of our school friends were there, and all the girls we knew and everything. We played about twenty songs, and we played the whole night. Two hours, then a break and two more. We went down really well."

Clark recalls, "We were terrible. But, all our mates were there, so it didn't matter." It mattered to Porteous. He left and was replaced by another set of brothers, Greg and Mike Ellison.

In the ensuing months, more opportunities for the band to play live presented themselves. Mainly at youth clubs and private gatherings, with the occasional warm-up slot at one of the city's newly opened rock clubs like Bungy's, The Place, or The Top Ten. Clark remembers, "We played Greenlight at Morningside on a stage that was only four feet deep but plenty long. The two guys on each side are both doing different songs at the same time. Can you imagine, we're doing 'I'm Your Puppet' on one side of the stage and the other two guys are playing 'Soul Man' … unbelievably bad." Those opening slots were for some of the biggest local beat groups including the Poets, the Beachcombers with Dave Paton (a future member of the Rollers and Pilot), and the Hipple People. "No guys wanted to see us. It was all girls. The guys would boo us off the stage. They were there for the Hipple People, not the Saxons."

These not-so-pleasant club experiences steeled the group's resolve and reinforced the idea that image would be key to the success of the Saxons. With a look that could be loosely described as "mod," the band took the stage wearing its own well-thought-out uniform. Says Alan, "We had our own look even then. Paper collars and ties, checked trousers."

Clark adds, "It was very conscious … the look. We were trying to carve out our own thing. My mother had a sewing machine, and Alan and I would go buy the fabric to make our own trousers, shirts, and jackets. It was like a little rock 'n' roll sweatshop. And a great feeling to be makin' our own stuff. Quite a buzz. Short jackets were all the rage, and we would add a bit of frill. They were very colorful. Lots of green satin … salmon and pink." With things cooking in the fashion department, the group continued to rehearse every night that they weren't booked to play a gig.

"Every night," remembers Alan, "there was no time for anything else. My schoolmates would egg me on and say 'Come on, we're going dancing tonight,' and I would say, 'No, I've got to stay in and practice with the band.' Guys would say 'He's wasting his time playing guitars when he could go out and have a good time.' But for us, it was always like, no, we can just stay and learn one more song."

It was during one of those evening rehearsals that the band made the first of many historic decisions. Attributing the lack of regular gigs to many factors—among them the group's relative inexperience—and with a renewed emphasis on image, it was decided that another name change was needed. Says Clark, "American music was really taking off in the clubs, and we felt it would be cool to have a name that reflected that vibe. For a laugh, Derek stuck a pin in the map of the USA on the wall."

Alan continues the story. "It ended up in some crappy place. I don't know where it was, some stupid name. And we stuck it in again and it landed on Bay City. A few more times, and that was still the best sounding of them all."

According to Clark, the moniker wasn't complete at that point. "We were actually going to call the band 'the Bay City Stompers.' In fact, that *was* it. Then Alan said he thought Rollers was better cause it was kind of like the Detroit Wheels."

The rock history books have recounted this story in various forms over the years, and it has always been reported that young Derek's pin landed squarely on Bay City, *Michigan*. But was it really? Carol Strauss-Klenfner, who headed the Rollers' U.S. publicity firm, "CJ Strauss," recalls it this way: "I remember asking about the origins of the group's name and pointing out to their manager that were, like, four cities in the States with that name, and for story-telling purposes, we'd need to figure out which one it was. Bay City, Michigan, was the winner because it was the biggest, had a decent-sized airport, was centrally located, and was easier to get in and out of than the other Bay Cities. You know, just in case we might ever have to go there. Eventually, they were invited there and got awarded a key to the city by the mayor on 'Bay City Rollers Day' in Bay City, Michigan. More hysteria there. A huge turnout. And I have often wondered if Bay City native Madonna was one of the little girls in the crowd. Anyway, sorry to the Rollers fans in Bay City, Texas. I guess it coulda been you."

With a new name and a renewed spirit, the band pulled a few strings to garner an audition at Edinburgh's hottest nightspot, the Top Story Club. Alan Longmuir says it was the huge break the band needed. "We kept going to see the guy at the Top Story, and he finally agreed to give us a spot during the break time between bands. It was packed right to the door. The heat was incredible. Unbelievable, the sweat and the smell. The place was a dump, but it had that rock and roll atmosphere, you know."

With a huge crowd there for the Hipple People, the newly christened Bay City Rollers ripped into their audition number, "Jump Back Baby." The performance was greeted with mass indifference. Most used the time to get to the bathroom or get a drink. The only exceptions were the twenty girls up front who had came to show their support during this crowning moment, and the manager of the headlining Hipples, Edinburgh bandleader and local celebrity Thomas "Tam" Paton.

Tam Paton, the son of an Edinburgh potato merchant, had been the leader of Edinburgh show band "the Crusaders," whose claim to fame was placing seventh in a London talent competition that had been judged by the likes of Ringo Starr, Beatles manager Brian Epstein, and his protégé, Cilla Black. Seventh place out of eight contestants did not sit well with Paton. He felt that they had sounded better than any of the other acts. Discouraged, he squeezed his way through the crowd of Beatles fans to ask Epstein directly why they had scored so low. The manager's response was to the point: "You are a wonderful band. A wonderful cover band. I heard no originality, and you have no image. Sorry."

Those were comments that would stay with Paton from that moment on. "Up to that point I thought it was all about sound. I realized then how important image was." Paton returned to Edinburgh and the Palais de Danse, where he led his big band with an Eppy-inspired emphasis on image. "I switched immediately from boring suits to brown mohair, big bowties, and topped it all off with a Tony Curtis hairdo. Our singer, Pat Fernie, put Dusty Springfield to shame with her voice and makeup. Image became everything." However, even with the new image, the writing was on the wall for Paton and his ilk. The big bands were out, and the beat was in. Paton knew it. "Personally, I knew I was a crap singer and a crap piano player. But, I did have the ability to organize and get gigs, so I focused my attention that way." It was at that point that he started to book younger bands for teen night at the Palais.

For the Bay City Rollers, being booked at the Top Story Club was the Holy Grail. Four flights up, with a stage made from snooker tables, the Top Story was Edinburgh's hottest rock club. Run by the Craig family, it was manager Jimmy Craig who was approached by Alan Longmuir and Greg Ellison looking for work. "Hey mister! Can ya make us famous?" asked Ellison.

"What's the name of your group?" snorted Craig.

Longmuir told him, and the not-surprising reply from Craig was, "Bay City Rollers? Achh, I've never heard of you."

Tam Paton, who was standing next to Craig, spoke up, "I've heard of them."

Alan remembers, "I turned around and saw who it was who said that, and I nearly fell down the stairs. Tam Paton was big time. He knew everybody on the circuit."

Derek concurs. "He was the most important manager in Edinburgh, even then. Everyone who wanted to play in a group was trying to meet him." Paton had remembered the Bay City Rollers from their previous Top Story audition and from seeing Alan and Derek at the side of the Palais stage watching other bands. He agreed on the spot to go to the Longmuir home to see the band rehearse.

After two "no-show" appointments, Paton finally made good on his promise with a 10 P.M. visit to the Longmuir home—much to the consternation of the elder Longmuirs, who worried what the neighbors may think of the volume coming from the small house at that late hour. He watched as the band worked its way through "Please Mister Postman" and "Hold On I'm Coming," even though the performance was, in his words, "wretched." He agreed to help them get work. Dropping a not-so-subtle hint that Mike Ellison and his moustache needed to go. He did, and Tam was on the case. The first area that got his attention was teen night at the Palais. "We were not doing well with the fourteen to sixteen-year-olds, so we started to book some of the young bands, putting them on one side of the revolving stage. We got the Bay City Rollers in for four nights, and the girls were already starting to scream. Our show band drummer Neil Smith heard it and said 'What the hell is that all about?' Then it hit me … this is what Mr. Epstein meant. Image. Young and smelly." There were two notable gigs amongst the first few booked by Paton for his new charges: sharing the bill at Rosewell Institute with the pre-Led Zeppelin Robert Plant and His Band Of Joy and another show with the Bee Gees. With the statute of limitations long expired, Nobby Clark comes clean with this admission: "I was knocked out by Barry Gibb's shirt. It was gold with puffy pirate sleeves, and I had to have it. I grabbed it in the dressing room and was heartbroken a year later when it was ripped to shreds from my body by an overzealous Rollers fan."

TWO

King for a Day,
but Not Much More

It was late 1969, and the death knell had sounded for Tam Paton and his band-leading days. "It was beat music first and foremost. But as far as the venues, the real nail in the coffin was bingo. That game single-handedly put the big bands out of business. There was nowhere to play, and nobody cared." It was just as well, because Paton found more and more of his time being spent on spreading the gospel of the Bay City Rollers, an exercise that was equal parts fascinating and frustrating. Financially, he was learning some tough lessons. Supplementing the band's operating coffers with money earned delivering potatoes for his Dad's business and a loan from local music storeowner Pete Seaton, Paton was realizing that keeping a rock group gigging didn't come cheap. One example being a Hammond B3 organ purchased by Paton for the band's keyboardist, Keith Norman (who had replaced Mike Ellison) in early 1970. "I had just put out £1,000 for the rig, Leslie speakers and all. Coming back from Aberdeen, he tells me he's out. I got one week's notice and never saw him or the organ again. Same old story ... girlfriend issues."

It was at this stage that Paton began to earn his reputation as a controlling Svengali. Paton says he had no choice. "I learned quite a lesson with Keith. Girlfriends are bad news for lots of rea-

19

sons. I literally had to tie up their nights with Chinese dinner whatever it takes to keep them focused. Don't let them fall in love. Without that dedication to purpose, it's disaster." It was a mantra that would eventually pay off—and then, some say, ultimately contribute to the band's demise.

Paton was also proving his mettle as a master of publicity with, among others, a stunt that involved paying kids to spray paint "Bay City Rollers" on the overpass of every major motorway. One such "billboard" was over the city's busy Princes Street. A photograph of it was printed in the *Daily News*, and it resulted in the band being brought up on charges. To make it right legally, the young Rollers were forced to go and clean it up, which of course ended up being another picture and story in the paper.

Meanwhile, gigs were becoming more plentiful, and the Bay City Rollers were starting to make a name for themselves on the Edinburgh scene. By the beginning of the new decade, the band had begun to write their own material. They'd also started introducing heavier numbers into their set list. The thought being that doing a few Cream, Sabbath, or Deep Purple songs might broaden their appeal a bit. It didn't. The audiences remained 85-90 percent female—at least partly by design. It was Paton who insisted on making the most of the female appeal of the band by demanding that the group not have girlfriends—at least, not publicly. The aura of inaccessibility was obviously working. "We had experimented with familiarity," says Clark, "and then we tried it the other way. It just worked better that way. The drill was get out of the van, on stage, do the set, leave. The idea at that early stage was to leave them wanting a bit more. No familiarity … and we got better and better at it. Other bands resented us for it. No, that's being nice. They hated us."

Derek Longmuir agrees, "It was that inaccessibility that made people want us even more." For these Rollers, it was all about the girls, and more and more of them were going out of their minds at the shows—a condition that didn't endear them any more to the males in the audience. Nobby Clark recalls, "There would be ten or twenty rows of girls, and behind them would be rows of guys hating us. Playing in Shotts there was a massive fight on the dance floor. A bunch of jealous guys went outside and smashed the windows in our van, cut up our tires. We had to drive all the way home on the rims."

Now becoming comfortable at the helm, Paton wielded his influence in other ways, most noticeably with matters involving personnel. Stung by the sudden departure of Norman, Paton decided to become more involved in the selection of band members, which resulted in an amazing amount of turnover in the Rollers ranks, a fact that Paton doesn't deny. "I didn't just ruthlessly push somebody down the road. Some people found it difficult because we were working like four or five nights a week, and they were falling off in terms of interest in the group. It's like putting a football team together. You have to have all winners." By mid-1970, the body count since the initial trio of the Longmuirs and cousin Neil Porteous was up to an incredible eleven members in five years and would grow by five more before the "classic" lineup was to take the stage for the first time in 1974. You could literally staff three more bands with ex-Bay City Rollers. Some were chosen for their obvious musical talent first (David Paton, Eric Faulkner) and others only for the all-important look and image (Eric Manclark, Neil Henderson). Nobby Clark was elated with the addition of David Paton. "Davy was a real musician, and his joining gave us a big boost. He could play lead guitar and sing great, which helped us pull off three-part harmonies that were needed to cover songs by the Beach Boys and Crosby, Stills, and Nash." Unfortunately, David's stay in the group was short lived, leaving the band, ironically, over his frustration with Tam's constant meddling with the band's line-up. The issue came to a head with the enlistment of Manclark. "Tam was delivering potatoes and saw Eric walking down the street. He approached him and asked 'Can you play a guitar?' Manclark said 'no,' and Tam says, 'Wanna be in a band?' It was maddening for anyone who was serious about the music, which Davy definitely was. It was just too much for him to take."

Looking back, Paton (the musician) did well by sticking to his guns. He, along with Billy Lyall, went on to much success with the band Pilot ("Magic," "January") and was a long time member of both the Alan Parsons Project and Elton John's band. He doesn't look back on his Rollers days with fond memories. "I probably learned something from it, but it's not something that I'm extremely proud of." Lyall would be the first to be asked to leave because of "boyfriend" rather than "girlfriend issues." According to Tam Paton, he and Derek were getting a bit "too close for comfort."

By the spring of 1971, the BCR lineup now featured the Longmuirs, Clark, Henderson, Manclark, and Archie Marr. It was this assemblage that had been seen late in 1970 on stage at Edinburgh's Cave's Club by industry veteran Tony Calder, Bell Records head Dick Leahy, and talent agent David Apps. Fogged in at the Glasgow airport and aware of the reaction the Rollers were getting; Calder's curiosity had been piqued despite being told by his close friend, concert promoter Ronnie Simpson, that the band was "rubbish" and a "waste of energy." The three (Calder, Leahy, and Apps) decided to go down and see what the fuss was all about. When they arrived, the Blair Street venue was packed and in full Rollers riot mode. After the show, Calder approached Paton, saying, "I want this band." The two met for tea, and Paton agreed to prove that the band had appeal outside of their hometown by doing a showcase in Dundee in early 1971. Calder agreed to bring a film crew and, if all went well, to sign the band to a production and development deal.

Leaving nothing to chance, Paton hired six buses and filled them with Edinburgh girls for the trip to Dundee. He need not have bothered; the Caves Club pandemonium was replicated at the Dundee ballroom, caught on film, and immediate plans were made to get the band to Barnes for a demo session at Olympia Studios.

Upon arriving in England, the cold reality of the situation had begun to kick in for Paton and the band. The advance money that Bell Records had paid Calder's company was nowhere to be found, and the sessions had been canceled. Tony Calder had, in

Paton's words, "… run cold on the boys. He was just too busy and lost interest as fast as he got that check."

That's when Dick Leahy stepped up and agreed to sign the band to a proper Bell Records contract without a demo. They had made an impression on Leahy that foggy night. "I really couldn't hear what they were playing or singing. All I could hear was this constant screaming." So, finally after six long years, it looked as if the Bay City Rollers ship had come in. However, it almost went back to sea before docking.

"It was a shit deal." That is Nobby Clark's recollection of the original contract offered to the band by Bell. "Dick Leahy had asked the band to come to London. They put us in a hotel and then gathered us round to sign our lives away." Everything was moving forward until discussion of the percentage clauses began. That's when Clark shocked Paton and his bandmates by stubbornly refusing to agree to the terms that were being presented. The deal being offered gave the band four percent of the net profits on any Bay City Rollers records. Clark, who had done some homework before making the trek to London, spoke up immediately. "I said look, I'm not happy with that part." And Leahy responded without blinking, "I didn't think you would be."

A twenty-four-hour stalemate ensued that almost resulted in Clark being replaced by an aggravated Paton. "I just thought, great, we've worked so hard to get here and now Nobby's fucked it up."

Clark remained true to his convictions. "Tam was very angry and threatened to get a lawyer after me." Sleeping on it paid off for all concerned, and, the next afternoon, a calmer Clark signed the revised contract that doubled the band's take to eight percent of net and gave them a £5,000 production advance.

Paton breathed a sigh of relief. "In the end he was right to do what he did," he remembers. "It sure took a hell of a lot to stand up to the big record company that way."

With the contract matter settled, Leahy and the brain trust at Bell went to work. The decision was made to bring in eccentric producer Jonathan King. The self-proclaimed "King of Hits,"

King had produced a handful of them for other artists and had even gone top five with his own 1965 single, "Everyone's Gone to the Moon." He seemed like a logical choice to work with the young band. Clark wasn't so sure. "He gave me the creeps. You don't really work with him anyway. He tells you what to do, and you do it."

Or, King would do it himself. "They couldn't really sing, so I made Nobby copy my lead vocal note for note, and inflection for inflection," King says. "I then sang all thirteen backing vocals, multi tracked. So, actually 'Keep On Dancing' is actually one Roller and thirteen J.K.'s."

Alan Longmuir felt stifled, saying of the period, "It was like being in the army. If they said jump, you jumped."

Tam Paton recalls that it was made very clear how things were going to be by King himself. "He said, 'I'm not farting about with a stupid fucking band. Just give me the singer.'"

Nobby remembers, "When I got there without the others, they were putting strings on. I went away for an hour, did the vocals. They mixed the next day, and that was it."

Four songs were produced and recorded by King. They included the planned first single, a cover of Tommy Roe's "We Can Make Music," and its intended follow-up, a remake of the Gentrys' "Keep On Dancing," plus two B-sides, "Alright" and "Jenny." The first pressings of "Music" b/w "Alright" have now become much sought after Rollers collectibles, as the decision was made to lead with "Keep On Dancing" instead. The original Leahy/King game plan was to record two more songs, but that would have required more than the allotted studio time and budget. Alas, we'll never hear how the Rollers would have handled the King-arranged "ooga-chaggas" in their version of the B.J. Thomas hit "Hooked On A Feeling." That honor went to King himself in December of '71, and, eventually, a note-for-note cover by Blue Swede hit the top ten in 1974.

"Keep On Dancing" was released in May, and most of the reviewers were kind. *Record Mirror's* Peter Jones said, "This is a very commercial record indeed. It's a pacey thing, with banks of vocal work from the six lads, a thudding bass figure, and a diabolically catchy arrangement all the way. A foot-tapper, folks. Honest, can't call it anything else. Sounds like a giant to me." With the single's release, the Rollers continued to play throughout Scotland, hoping all the while that their debut disc would fare well in England, where they were virtually unknown. Despite the mostly positive reviews, early indications were not good. In fact, it wasn't until Bell Records plugger and former Radio One presenter Chris Denning made it his number one promotion priority that the single showed any signs of life. Denning, a close friend of King's, would eventually be found guilty of sex offenses involving under-age boys and would also be linked to fellow convicted sex offenders King, Paton, and television presenter Matthew Kelly in the 2002 "Walton Hop" scandal.

With Denning putting the pressure on in ways one can only now imagine, the single finally debuted at number 24 in mid-September, four long months after it had been released. It eventually worked its way into the top ten, where it peaked at number 9 in early November, guaranteeing that they would be able to steam into 1972 with the momentum of a big debut hit. Radio presenter Dave Eager was one of the original believers. "I had originally played the first release of 'Keep On Dancing' on BBC Radio One. I believed that the Rollers could be stars. Afterwards I invited the Rollers to do a gig at The New Century Hall in Manchester. It was their first gig outside Scotland. Even though the Manchester audience had never ever seen The Rollers, they went down a storm...and I immediately got them three more bookings. I also made the chorus from the record a jingle for BBC Radio One Clubs, which I was presenting live throughout the U.K.. This kept the sound of the Rollers on the airwaves even though they had no current record. Eventually, as they built up a fan base, people became more aware of the jingle and started asking about it. Because I stuck with them, Tam promised that, come whatever, if and when they did a nationwide tour, I would be their compere. Tam kept his promise." For the band, it was time to learn a tough lesson.

They'd soon find out that it's harder to rekindle magic than make it, and that Jonathan King was well on his way to reaffirming his real reputation as the King of One-Hit Wonders … again.

THREE

Knee Tremblers
and Nobby Nights

So, how do you spend New Year's Eve following your con-quest of the top ten? For some acts, maybe a headlining spot on a big TV show, or a concert tour. If you were the Bay City Rollers on the last night of 1971, it was honoring your commitment to play for a half-empty room of middle-agers at a Bournemouth workingman's club. It would end up being an omen of hard times to come. But, buoyed by the success of "Keep On Dancing," the group's spirits remained high as they toured the country through the early part of '72, until it became obvious that "We Can Make Music" was not going to be the Rollers' follow up hit. Fresh out of Jonathan King-produced tunes, Dick Leahy made the decision to enlist the talents of song-writer/producer/managers Ken Howard and Alan Blaikely for the next BCR recordings.

The sessions resulted in five songs being cut, among them "In Love's Dominion" and "Manana." Howard and Blaikely came to the proceedings with a similar pedigree and way less personality issues than Jonathan King. They had been there before. The Hampstead duo were responsible for ten different top ten hits by Dave Dee, Dozy, Beaky, and Mick & Tich from 1965-68. They also were behind the Honeycombs' 1964 number-one hit

"Have I the Right?" and chart successes from Lulu, the Herd (Peter Frampton), and Petula Clark; they were even the first in the U.K. to write a hit for Elvis Presley ("I've Lost You"). So, the group's spirits were understandably high as they prepared their third single for release.

Even Nobby Clark—who had barely concealed his contempt for King—had brightened considerably with this effort. Helping the mood, no doubt, was the inclusion of the Clark-penned "Because I Love You" as the B-side of the "Manana" single; this served as the first acknowledgement by the brass at Bell of any Rollers talents beyond Nobby's hurried vocals and the rest of the band smiling during the photo shoots for the picture sleeves. "The vibe was good," recounts Clark. "We were busy traveling to different countries than we had ever been to. Staying in great hotels. It was fantastic for a little while." The band even used their newfound confidence to push the limits of Paton's regulations, earning Henderson the nickname of "Knee Trembler Neil" from members of the road crew for his side-of-the-stage sexual proclivities.

Things soon started to sour. The band, desiring to work more in England, had acquired the services of London agent Barry Perkins. Says Dave Eager, "Barry Perkins met the Rollers through me. Barry had been working originally at Kennedy Street Artistes in Manchester. Kennedy Street managed bands like 'Herman's Hermits,' 'The Mindbenders,' 'Freddie and the Dreamers,' and as I lived and disc jockeyed in Manchester and also had got work via Kennedy Street, I knew Barry. While working at Top Of The Pops in London as well as BBC Radio One, I also had made friends with groups including 'Marmalade,' 'The Tremeloes,'...and these bands were managed by a London-based guy who was well known in the business called Peter Walsh. I knew that Peter was one of the go getters...movers and shakers in the business. Barry had left Manchester and went to work for Peter Walsh. When the first smell of success started to happen for The Rollers and we were traveling down to London, Tam said they still didn't have anyone to look after them agency-wise. It was at that stage I mentioned Barry Perkins. I told Tam that Barry was a go-getter, but I added that he needed to be careful as London frequently 'eats' people! I called Barry and told him about Tam and gave him Tam's number. He met with Barry and within a few days had the band signed to his agency." According to Nobby Clark, that was a big mistake.

"They booked us in all the wrong places," says Clark. "We had a week-long engagement at this place called the Top Hat Club in Newcastle. It was a snooker club, and we were booed off the stage. The other acts on the bill were a comedian and a dog, and they went down great. I guess we should have had a parrot or something." The manager of the club, not pleased with the attitude of the discouraged Rollers and their crew, called Perkins, who in turn called Tam Paton, who proceeded to angrily confront his charges. "He comes down and starts screaming at us," continues Clark, "just rips us apart! I got right back in his face. I screamed at him don't you fucking start with me! We almost broke up the band right then and there."

The group continued to slog through a never-ending series of poorly attended English one-nighters. For Tam Paton, it meant more patented—or should that be "Paton-ted"—personnel changes; out went Archie Marr and Neil Henderson, replaced by John Devine and Eric Faulkner, members of an Edinburgh band called KIP that Paton had been thinking of managing, before he decided instead to use it as a Rollers farm club. Faulkner recalls the audition: "It was a pretty weird concept 'cause the band we were in was into Slade and T-Rex and that stuff." Undeterred by the contrast in influences, Paton insisted that the two give it a shot. "They [the Rollers] were like, so, what songs do you know? And we never knew anything that they were playing. I think we auditioned with a Mott the Hoople song or something." It worked. The longer haired, harder-rocking Faulkner and Devine were in, probably because of their edge. Says Eric, "I think that's why we got put in the band … to try and harden it up."

Eric Francis Falconer was born on October 21, 1953, one of two sons born to George and Frances Falconer of South

Edinburgh. His musical interests surfaced early on, when he studied the viola and played in the local school youth orchestra. By his early teens, inspired by the Shadows, he had taken up the guitar as well and had gotten his first paying job with a band called Witness at the age of thirteen. Leaving school a little later, after having passed his O-levels, he moved in with his Aunt Peggy after his parents left Edinburgh. He then joined a band called Sugar, which was to become KIP and changed the spelling of his last name to Faulkner for showbiz purposes.

On the road, the band toyed with a new image. Faulkner experimented with shortened trousers and Doc Martens boots, hoping to move the band's look into an area that might get attention from the younger audience that had started to desert the group in droves since they'd adopted the bow tie and cabaret jacket look. "I thought, we've got to do something, and it was just an idea that worked. It helped us stand out when we got on TV." The tartan was soon added, and "Roller Gear" was slowly being introduced.

Jake Duncan, who would eventually become the Rollers road manager, first started to work with the band at this time. He remembers, "The first shows were amazing. I would set up the drums and our WEN PA system. The other roadie, Davy Purdy, would stay on one the side of the stage, and I'd be on the other. He gave me great advice at the first show: 'Anything goes wrong … fix it.' So we're watching the gig, and a piece of the drum set starts to go and I hear Davy yell 'fix it!' So, I go running on stage, only to have Eric—who I'd just met that afternoon—boot me with the top of his shoe. I'll never forget what he said to me: 'Off the stage, guffie.' He hadn't spoken two words to me all day, and now he was making things very clear. I fixed the problem and got off Eric's stage. Then, after the show, I'm putting away the drum rig and earnestly thinking, 'Well, I've made it through the first one,' when along comes this girl who yells at me, 'Hey you! My sister wants to bang you!' I was pretty sure I knew what she meant, but I just put my head down and finished with the drums. Davy let me have it after that. He said, 'Jake, that is half the reason to take this job.' That's how I learned about the fringe benefits of being on tour with the Bay City Rollers."

According to Duncan, desperation was becoming obvious within the band's ranks. "We were now playing what I call the 'has been, haven't been' circuit. This was after 'We Can Make Music' and 'Manana' had both stiffed. We would do weekends in England, leave Thursday and back on Sunday. The band was pretty close to being ready to call it a day. To show you how desperate we were, we actually took bookings in Northern Ireland, which was a sure sign of a band that needed the money. That was not a safe place to be in those days, but it was necessary to pay the bills."

On the U.K. charts, the absence of the Bay City Rollers grew longer. "Manana" was not living up to expectations, even though it had placed in the Luxembourg Grand Prix song contest and had garnered them some good international television exposure, charting in Holland, Germany, and Finland. It even went to number one in Israel of all places. The song was ultimately a failure where it mattered most, at home. No amount of Chris Denning promotion was going to save it, and it sank almost as fast as it was released in Britain. To say that panic was setting in at this point would be an understatement. Once again, a change in producers was suggested.

The decision was made to ignore the other four Blaikely/Howard tracks and bring in the third Rollers production team in a year and a half. This time, the call went out to the writing/producing team of Bill Martin and Phil Coulter, who'd met the band in Luxembourg and had stayed in touch since. Like the others before them, Martin and Coulter boasted an impressive resume, including hits by Cliff Richard, Elvis Presley, the Troggs, Cilla Black, and their biggest, a number one with "Puppet On A String" by Sandie Shaw.

The pair was just as "hands on" as Jonathan King had been, but came off decidedly differently due to Glasgow-native Martin's "Scots" attitude—which was appreciated by Paton, who felt he needed someone to align with for moral support. He got it from Martin and from Irishman Coulter, who assured Paton that they had the right material for the band this time around. They would work through year's end to be ready with a new BCR sound for 1973.

The Bay City Rollers convened at Mayfair Studio to tackle the decidedly upbeat Martin/Coulter compositions. On the docket were four songs: "Saturday Night," "Hey CB," "Shang A Lang," and "Remember." Using the same modus operandi as King and Blaikley/Howard before them, the only Rollers requested to actually appear on tape would be singer Nobby Clark. "I remember thinking the songs were stronger with these guys. Plus Mayfair was just a cooler scene. They used Gary Glitter's handclaps (two pieces of wood) on all the tracks, and it just came across fresh." The change was evident in the sound of the first single from the sessions.

Bill Martin explains, "The song 'Saturday Night' was unusual as Phil was ill and not at the session. I had one of our staff writers with me, Big John Drummond, who could play a guitar. We had written the song like an American cheerleader song like O-H-I-O. OHIO! When it came to the piece where the band chants 'S-A-T-U-R-D-A-Y NIGHT' they speed up. I had no idea they were getting faster and sounding more Scottish than ever. Christ, I'm Scottish! How was I to know?"

The decision was made to release the song as the first single, and, once again, all involved crossed their fingers. "I was getting excited," says Martin. "I played it to Dick [Leahy], who said he would run with it, and it flopped. Dick nevertheless thought we were the right combination—he was correct." As for the spelling lesson on vinyl that was "Saturday Night," it would take two years, a new vocal track, and a trip across the Atlantic to prove Martin right. However, in the U.K. in early 1973, it was just another in a disturbing series of stiffs for the Bay City Rollers— a string of disappointment that had not gone unnoticed by Bell. Dick Leahy phoned Tam Paton and requested his immediate presence at the label's London office for an urgent meeting. For Cinderella, it was getting close to midnight.

FOUR

One Last Kick at the Ball

When Tam arrived at the Bell Records office, he fully expected the band to be released from their contract due to their inability to follow up "Keep On Dancing." What he got instead was an ultimatum from Leahy: the label was prepared to release one more single, but that would be it. If it didn't connect, Bell would have no choice but to cut their losses and move on. Thankful for the opportunity to have "one last kick at the ball," Paton hurried back to Edinburgh to rally the troops and let them know that this was it. "Remember" would be the band's only chance for redemption. When Tam arrived home, the group was begrudgingly preparing to head back to the war zone that was Northern Ireland. They left for the road with the assurance from their manager that he was going to do "Whatever I could to make sure that 'Remember' was a hit."

The band wasn't as optimistic. One member had made his mind up already. "I was leaving," says Nobby Clark. "On my twentieth birthday, I had already made up my mind that I had to get out. I was thinking of getting married, plus I was into a kind of American West Coast thing, Neil Young, Jackson Browne, CSN, America. It just wasn't where the rest of the band, especially Eric, was at. The Rollers sound just wasn't appealing to me at all anymore. Plus, I was unhappy being that controlled."

Clark vowed to finish up the Irish dates and then be done with it all. Faulkner tried to discourage him, saying, "You've got to be mad. This is the biggest mistake you'll ever make." But Clark remained true to his convictions and served notice to the rest that he was leaving in November.

Northern Ireland was not a safe haven by any stretch. But, for the BCR it was one of the few places where they had truly turned the corner with the audience. The reaction the band got there was much closer to the scenes of Rollermania that were to come: screaming, fainting, and long lines at the sold-out theaters. Looking back, it is debatable that much of this was due to the complete lack of competition for the teenage Irish girls' rock and roll release and adulation. Whatever ... it was working, and Jake Duncan remembers that first feeling of Irish success. "The band was using a Mercedes 408 to travel when I started. Eventually they had gotten a decent PA and an Econoline van. One would haul the lights and the other the backline and PA. I wanted to know why we hadn't any sleeping bags or blankets for the trip, and Tam said, 'Just leave it running and use the heater' without any worries for the petrol situation. I thought, 'Well, that's it, I've arrived.'" For his efforts, Duncan received the princely sum of £8 per week. But he made it work, using this as his motto: "All you can eat, give Derek the receipt," laughs Jake.

The band didn't escape without a few dicey moments on the road in the land of "the troubles." Jake Duncan recalls one particular instance: "I remember leaving Londonderry and getting completely lost. Which at the time, was not a good thing. These guys were at war and would do things like turn street poles with the town names around like 180 degrees just to confuse people. We came to a sign that said 'Port Rush straight ahead' when, in fact, we should have turned right. That sort of thing. We were irretrievably lost. Everybody is well locked up in his or her houses, it is the dead of night, and we have absolutely no idea where we are. We pulled over to the side of the road and started looking at a map through the light of the windscreen. All of a sudden, the total quiet is broken by the sound of engines revving. Three Land Rovers come flying up. 'Stand back from the vehicles' they shouted. 'Do not move.' They stopped about thirty yards away and started checking us out with searchlights. Two or three minutes later, after we had convinced them we were a pop group that was lost, they were gone. In that short amount of time, it had gone from total silence to all the commotion back to silence again. I remember saying 'Look, *these people* don't want to be here, so why do we want to be here?' It was very frightening and deathly quiet at 3 A.M. But in the long run it was great ... Ireland was like our second home."

Back in Preston Pans, Tam Paton, fresh from his meeting with Bell Records, had devised a plan to get the word out about the "Remember" single. "I had managed to get my hands on a David Cassidy fan club book of some sort, and then there was a magazine called *Swapshop* ... from those I lifted names and addresses of the kids writing in to swap for pictures of Donny Osmond or David Cassidy or whatever. I sent picture postcards of the band to every one of these David Cassidy fans and these kids writing in to *Swapshop*. I sent out loads and loads of these postcards. In fact, I borrowed five hundred pounds from my parents for the postage alone. At that time the stamps were about two and a half pence, so you can imagine how many cards we sent away. I sent these cards everywhere. I sent them to DJ's, to television producers, to everybody. That picture went out everywhere. My mother, her friends, myself, we sat down and did all that ourselves. We posted away thousands of these cards." The postcards, a hastily assembled collage of the group members' faces, included the following call to action in bold capital letters: **REMEMBER ... BUY YOUR COPY TODAY**.

Then, a funny thing happened on the way to obscurity: Paton's plan began to work. "Remember" was picking up steam and just about to go into the charts when Nobby Clark's predetermined date of departure arrived. Paton had been so consumed with getting the record played that he hadn't quite taken Clark's departure as seriously as he should have. That changed immediately when, with the group on the way to a gig in Perth, Clark's moment came: "I'm not going. I'm done." Paton picks up the tale from there. "I had seen Les McKeown in a band called Threshold one night in Dunbar with Eric Faulkner. I had asked him if he'd ever consider joining the band. With Nobby leaving, we made up our mind right there and then to get him into the group. I literally turned the car around and grabbed him for the gig that night."

Leslie Richard McKeown (b. 11.12.55) was the youngest of Frank and Florence McKeown's four boys. Raised in the predominantly Irish Broomhouse district of Edinburgh, the young McKeown got the rock and roll bug, like the others, at around the age of fifteen. Soon after, he took it upon himself to advertise for a band to front in the *Edinburgh Evening News*. The ad resulted in a phone call from Alan Wright, who said that his band Threshold needed a singer. Asked if he had any experience, McKeown lied and said that he had and was hired on the spot. It was a bold move that demonstrated a steely nerve that would be seen many times in the heady days to come. It was that nerve and overall attitude that really sold Tam Paton on his new singer. "Les brought in a freshness. He was cheeky and outspoken. The cherry on top of the cream cake."

McKeown got through the first gig with his new band thanks to Jake Duncan taping pieces of paper with song lyrics all over the stage for Les to read. The next day, February 1, it was off to London for an appearance on the live children's TV show *Crackerjack*. When the band arrived at the Shepherd's Bush Empire, they discovered that the broadcast had been canceled at the last minute due to a BBC workers union strike. Frustrated, the group started back to the van for the trip back to Scotland. Just then, a call came in through the theater stage door for Paton, requesting that the band stay in London to appear on *Top of the Pops*, since it looked like they might be in the top forty soon with "Remember." It was Friday night. *TOTP* recorded on Wednesdays. The group made the most of the intervening four days. At Mayfair, Les recut the vocals for "Remember," "Shang A Lang," and "Saturday Night." The new version of "Remember" was quickly sent to the pressing plant so that the shops would have copies of the record with the proper lead vocalist. Then, on

Tuesday, while McKeown was whisked away to record the "live vocal" for the TV show, Faulkner and Bill Martin went to work on acquiring the clothes that the band would wear on this momentous occasion. The band had appeared on *TOTP* back in '71, but that was well before Eric had joined, and he was intent on doing his part to be sure that they made a better visual impact this time.

On February 7, 1974, exactly ten years to the day after the Beatles had arrived in America, all of Britain got their first peek at the new-look Bay City Rollers. Faulkner and producer Martin's shopping spree had resulted in matching red football jerseys with white numbers, skin-tight white trousers shortened to mid-calf, and boots with the "biggest stack heels we could get our hands on." All of the group had undergone a quick haircut and adopted a variation of a modified shag style administered by Eric "Vidal Sasson" Faulkner.

The end result was the break the band had been waiting for. Within hours, the phone in Tam Paton's Paddington hotel room began to ring. First up was Bell Records' Leahy with encouraging words, and then agent and soon-to-be business manager Barry Perkins, who shared his excitement and the news that his office line was ringing off the hook. They were on the chart at week's end, debuting at number 38. One month later, it was another performance on *TOTP*, and this time they went before the cameras with the confidence of having the number six song in the country. It was a time to rejoice. Especially for the newest Roller, sixteen-year-old Stuart John "Woody" Wood (b. 2.25.57), who replaced a burned out John Devine to finalize what would become known as the "classic" BCR lineup. Leahy was sold at this point. "From then on, you knew they were going to be big. You didn't know how big, but you certainly knew they were going to be successful and that it wouldn't be just one hit." There wasn't much time to enjoy all of the good news. The fame train had arrived, and it was leaving the station in a hurry.

FIVE

Rollin' in It

Guitarist Stuart "Woody" Wood spent his seventeenth birthday at the home of his parents, John and Joan Wood, pinching himself over his good fortune. Like Eric Faulkner and John Devine before him, he had been a member of KIP and a band called "Wot's Up." Tam Paton had talked to him about the possibility of someday joining the Rollers. With Devine's abrupt departure, someday came sooner than anyone could have imagined. He was a Bay City Roller, having joined the band at the precise moment that they were about to explode in popularity. Although more than proficient at his instrument, Wood knew the real deal: "I'm sure my being asked to join the Rollers had a lot to do with image. The way I looked definitely was more important to Tam than how I could play. I could play, but mind you, I was only sixteen."

With the pace now picking up considerably, the seeds of Rollermania that had been planted with earlier appearances were starting to sprout into a full-blown scene across the country. "We were booked into a big hall in Sunderland," says Paton. "A mile away we start seeing all these kids with tartan scarves. I figured there must be a football match. We started to unload the equipment, and it turned into a riot right there in the street."

Promoters began asking Perkins for an extra security clause to be inserted into the band's engagement contracts.

Bell released the next Rollers single, "Shang A Lang," and this time there was no waiting around or gnashing of teeth. It stormed its way onto the chart at number 35 following the group's April 18 *Top of the Pops* appearance. *TOTP* was one of many television turns that the suddenly white-hot Rollers were to make, including Granada TV's *Lift Off* hosted by Ayshea Brough and produced by Muriel Young, the previously canceled *Crackerjack*, *The Basil Brush* (an annoying fox) *Show*, and *Blue Peter*. The exposure catapulted "Shang A Lang" into the top five by mid-May, selling 630,000 copies a day at its peak; it ultimately made it to number 2 on the chart with only the Rubettes' "Sugar Baby Love" denying them the top spot for the first time. The teen magazines that had been devoting most of their covers and space to David Cassidy and the Osmonds were now featuring the Rollers in their place.

The group recorded four more songs with Martin/Coulter: "Summerlove Sensation," "All of Me Loves All of You," "Bringing Back the Good Times," and "The Bump."

As plans were being made to begin work on the band's first album, Bell rush-released "Summerlove Sensation," which was bulleting to the number 3 spot on the chart while an already overwhelmed Paton and Perkins began discussing the band's first full scale U.K. concert tour. They would play larger venues than they had ever attempted before. Meanwhile, as they made good on bookings made prior to *Top of the Pops*, in every city— Glasgow, Edinburgh, Newcastle, Manchester, Birmingham—the scene was the same: bedlam. Rollermania was sweeping Britian. The front pages featured photographs of girls who had passed out, bobbies holding back the sea of tartan-bedecked bodies who all had to get a piece of their favorite Roller. A rush to the stage at an open-air concert in Harlow resulted in barricades being toppled, and many of the over 10,000 in attendance—and security—ending up in a pond that separated the audience from the stage. Dave Eager remembers those first signs of "Rollermania" at the shows. "In Halifax, which is a small town in Yorkshire

England, we arrived at the venue to hear noises from under the stage. It turned out that two girls had been hiding under the stage for over twenty-four hours just so they could sneak into the gig and be with the Rollers. This came as a surprise to everyone, no one expected it! The atmosphere was of mild hysteria which grew throughout the tour but, because this was on an upwards spiral, everyone was able to grow along with it. However, there were some crowd control problems as many of the venues were not designed for any sort of mania. The tour promoter, Jef Hanlon—Rock Artistes Management—I think the company was called and myself developed a system whereby I would have three levels of crowd control. Because the majority of the fans were young and excitable, I had to speak....chat with them from the stage as though we were all 'in it together.' Some of the gigs had no seats....so the fans sat on the floor but of course as soon as the Rollers came on....the fans stood up and rushed the stage. This caused crushing and the ones at the back could not see. Every so often Jef would get the message to me to get the Rollers off, I would have to go on and calm down the audience...then bring the Rollers back on. The police and security also didn't really appreciate what was happening which is probably why *Melody Maker* wrote about me being the 'Magician of Pantomine fame'...as I used to go on and get the fans to sit down again! I could never get over the aftermath of the shows. To put it mildly, the theatres 'smelled.' The aftermath of the mass hysteria was seats that were broken and dripping wet with urine, torn pieces of clothing and scattered gifts which had been thrown everywhere." By all accounts, it was a war zone.

Paton tried to explain the phenomenon: "I've always recognized there's been a massive vacuum. The Woodstock era has gone completely. And it's left behind a massive vacuum of kids— I wouldn't even say kids, I'd say people—all different kinds of people. And they're looking for something new. And they've grabbed on to the Rollers." With the incredible amount of coverage the band was getting came the inevitable first wave of negative press. Not a complete backlash (that would come later), but a few newspaper pieces here and there criticizing the group for their look and musical dependence on Martin and Coulter.

Eric Faulkner, the thinnest-skinned of the band, responded in kind. "It doesn't worry us. It just seems unprofessional on the part of whoever is knocking us. We've not gone around slagging other bands off. There are fans for all types of music. We've never said we were the greatest band in the world musically. We go on learning like everyone else."

Privately, Faulkner was fuming over the label's unwillingness to allow the group to write the B-sides of their singles. Faulkner and Wood had begun to write together, and Eric could not understand why Bell wouldn't allow them to have an avenue for that creativity.

Martin and Coulter wouldn't budge. When it came to the forthcoming LP, they wanted all three singles plus the next, "All Of Me Loves All Of You," the four B-sides, and the re-recorded "Saturday Night," leaving room for one BCR original. Eric came unglued, threatening to leave the band if that arrangement wasn't addressed and changed in a hurry. After a few tense meetings, it was agreed that the band would indeed be allowed to include four of its own compositions on the LP, to be called Rollin'.

Worn out, the band decided to take a quick holiday before starting work on the album. Tam, Woody, and Derek flew to Jamaica, Eric and Alan went home, and Les took his parents to the south of France for a much-deserved break. It was one of very few they would get over the next three years of whirlwind activity. The Rollers convened at Mayfair Studios in August to record the remaining tracks for their maiden LP. The compromise from earlier allowed the band to supplement the six Martin/Coulter compositions with two covers, "Be My Baby" and "Please Stay," and four originals: "Angel Angel," "Just a Little Love," "Ain't it Strange," and "There Goes My Baby." They would be given a grand total of six days to complete the task.

Barely past his aggravation over the non-inclusion of his songs, Eric Faulkner railed again over the short amount of time that the group was given to record. And the fact that, again, studio musicians who included, among others, drummer Clem

Cattini and guitarist Chris Spedding had already recorded most of the backing tracks. Faulkner finished the sessions under protest and once again asked for a summit meeting with Paton and Perkins. This time the frustrations felt by the young guitarist were taken more to heart, and Tam promised to sort it all out with Bell during their upcoming contract renegotiations.

The band had a year to go on their existing deal. Bell Records and the Columbia-Screen Gems labels (Colpix, Colgems, etc.) were renamed Arista Records. The former president of Columbia Records, Clive Davis, was running the new label. The Bell artists would either be let go, or would be taken over by Arista. Bell's early 1970s mainstay artists Dawn (with Tony Orlando) signed with Elektra, and the Fifth Dimension went to ABC. Others were dropped. During this period of transition, promising rock and roll artists such as Suzi Quatro and Hot Chocolate were farmed out to Big Tree. Hot Chocolate's "Emma," which was originally on Bell, eventually made top ten on Big Tree in early 1975. Potential big pop moneymakers Barry Manilow and Melissa Manchester went to Arista. With the Rollers future at Arista up in the air, these meetings would determine the group's recording future for years to come. Also on Paton's plate were publishing and merchandising deals. Creatively and financially, it was the most critical time in the group's history. And Tam Paton would soon blow it all in the most spectacular of ways.

Sensing the incredible demand, Bell began accepting pre-sale orders for *Rollin'* in mid-September. By the time it was available in early October, there was no denying that it would be a huge hit. The album entered the official British album chart at number one, something that had never happened before, blazing past Paul McCartney and Wings' *Band on the Run* and Mike Oldfield's *Tubular Bells* to grab the top spot. It would stay there through Christmas and would remain on the chart for an incredible sixty-two weeks total, a record eventually eclipsed by Pink Floyd's *Dark Side of the Moon*.

The Bay City Rollers were flying in rare air. "All of Me Loves All of You," after a slow start, ended up being their fourth straight top five single. Fan club membership was at an all time high of over 40,000 and was growing by 2,000 a day. The band was about to get its own monthly magazine and daily Granada TV show. Former Beatles press agent Tony Barrow was enlisted for similar duties, and Jef Hanlon was tabbed to promote their biggest tour to date. The new brain trust met at Paton's parents' home to prepare for what was to come. Reinforcing the road efforts would be a new PA, lighting rig, vans, security team, hairdressers, tailors, and a beefed-up road crew. Jake Duncan, now officially the band's tour manager, recalls, "It was all a big improvement. Which happens when you've gone from playing for 200 to 20,000."

On October 11, 1974, the band made their eighth *Top of the Pops* appearance in as many months. Alan Longmuir was beginning to feel the strain. "Some pop people buy Rolls-Royces. I'm happy with my new fiberglass fishing rod. Trouble is, I never get time to use it. Sometimes I wish it would all just stop, so I could go out my own front door, walk down the street to look at the shops, then come home quietly and watch telly like anybody else."

One week away from the beginning of the tour, the now self-described "sixth Bay City Roller," Paton, was in his element, putting the BCR publicity machine's proverbial pedal to the metal. Doing interviews for anyone with a notepad or tape recorder, the manager (not the band members) hammered home various themes of wholesomeness with the fervor of a political PR man. The oft-repeated themes being, in no particular order:

They don't drink alcohol (even though the *Rollin'* album inside sleeve featured a Q&A where, when asked their favorite drink, the band members mention vodka, rum, and cointreau).

They drink milk ... lots and lots of milk (evidenced by the pitchers of the stuff made evident on the table at every press conference).

They don't smoke (even though Les's "Marlboro minutes" were how time-outs at TV tapings were described
at the time) and can't stand girls who do. And on the subject of females ...

None of them has a girlfriend because they just do not
have time, and it wouldn't be fair (not a peep from the
girlfriends of McKeown, Faulkner, or Alan Longmuir).

While the teen magazines took to repeating these myths
word for word, the "serious" rock press began to turn a bit nas-
tier. Elton John was among those who were already tiring of the
hype: "I'm fed up with having them thrust down my throat in all
the papers. Every day it's 'Bay City Rollers Cat Gets Cold' or
'Man Runs Off With Bay City Rollers' Dog'." Many articles
accused the group of orchestrating the scenes of mania and inciting crowds to hysteria. Criticism of the group's "choirboy"
image and "simple" music began to appear more and more frequently.

No matter, there were other headlines to be written. The
twenty-six-city tour began with an incredible scene in
Birmingham. Just after quitting time, a truck broke down on one
of the city's thoroughfares, causing a major traffic backup. As
"luck" would have it, the Rollers were in the middle of it all,
stuck inside a van on their way to Birmingham Town Hall for
sound check. As word got out to the Rollers fans lined up outside the venue that their heroes were just up the road and sta-
tionary, all manner of hell broke loose, ensuring that "Roller
Fans Riot Stops City Traffic" would be plastered across the front
page the next morning. Beyond the crowds and scenes of pandemonium, it had become clear that the group's look was connect-
ing in a way never seen before in pop music. With Paton pushing the "we like girls who dress like us" angle, the fans responded by attending the shows completely bedecked in "Roller Gear,"
a fact that was not lost on the merchandisers, authorized and
otherwise, who began churning out as much tartan-trimmed
clothing as possible: pants, shirts, jackets, and even official Bay

City Rollers platform shoes. The shows were a sea of Scot's plaid. Rosettes and scarves were held aloft as the tears ran down the faces of the thousands of screaming girls who attended the shows. Rollermaniacs dressed to please to the tune of over £250,000 in gross receipts for the band for their one month on the British road. Good work if you can get it. And there was more where that came from. But who would be doing the profiting? As the band finished the year with shows in Ireland and Germany, they had quite a bit to ponder.

Time for those meetings. Accountant Stephen Goldberg convinced Paton and Perkins at this point that the best thing to do for the group's financial future was to devise a system wherein the band's income would be disbursed throughout an intricate structure of thirteen companies, all falling under the parent umbrella of Bay City Rollers Ltd.

The move was made to at least on the surface to ease the band's tax liability now that they were earning so much more. One of those companies, Bay City Music, was set up for publishing songs written by the band. It would be administered by a London-based publishing entity, Carlin Music. New York attorney Marty Machat began the task of renegotiating the contract with Bell/Arista after pocketing $50,000 for the honor of doing so. The new company was dropping most of the Bell acts. Tony Roberts, who replaced Dick Leahy at Bell, wanted to be sure the Rollers stayed on the new label, and he wanted Machat to know it as they readied for a new BCR single and album in January 1975. On the tenth anniversary of the group forming, their biggest U.K. hit and first trip to America were still to come.

By the time "All of Me Loves All of You" had peaked, the Rollers had, to a man, become disenfranchised with the Martin/Coulter production arrangement. Even Paton voiced his displeasure with what all perceived as a formula that needed to change, saying, "We need better material." And then, with a nod to Faulkner's consternation, "I think the boys themselves can write better than that." With Tony Roberts's backing—and a lovely parting gift (check) from Arista—Bill and Phil were o-u-t after *only* producing four top-five singles and a number-one album.

Martin says, "We cut a commercial deal with Clive for our release as producers and wished him all the best, ostensibly they [the Rollers] were history to us from that date." Ending their relationship with the BCR didn't keep them out of the charts. "We had cut a song with the Rollers that ended up as a B-side for them called 'The Bump.' As we had no group, Phil and I record-ed this as 'Kenny,' and suddenly we were number two with no band. So, we created one. I always thought, and so did Les McKeown, that this should have been released as a Bay City Rollers single. It would have been number one in the States." Martin remembers the parting of ways with the band as not being very cordial. "They were belligerent, unhappy, jealous, and a complete pain." As to their own songwriting abilities at the time, he scoffs, "I don't think they could have rhymed moon and June." He wasn't the only one saying that. What started out as a minor criticism of the group was turning into a full-fledged scandal.

"Bay City Rollers Don't Play Instruments!"

That was the accusation being thrown at the band in the British papers at the dawn of the New Year. Even though they had disproved this statement with hundreds of gigs over the years, it was, for the most part, true when it came to the studio. The band adopted an official position that they would publicly downplay what had come before and prove to the world that although studio "help" had been made available in the past, all future recordings would feature the band themselves playing and singing virtually every note. And the man who would oversee this recording breakthrough would be Irishman Phil Wainman.

Like the previous BCR producers before him, Wainman had enjoyed quite a career before working with the group. His first group, the Paramounts, morphed into Procol Harum ("Whiter Shade of Pale"), then he began to make a name for himself as a much-in-demand session drummer. Then, in the late 60s, while a member of the group the Quotations, he started writing songs with Johnny Goodison. That partnership would bear fruit in years to come with the Rollers and the band Mud. But what really put Wainman on the map and on the Bay City Rollers "producer wish list" was his work behind the board for the Sweet and their glam-rock hits, including "Blockbuster," "Wig Wam Bam," "Little Willy," "Teenage Rampage," and "Ballroom Blitz." It was a tougher, more guitar-oriented sound that the Rollers hoped to emulate.

The group had a great first meeting with Wainman on their home turf in Edinburgh in January. They made it clear to him that they were absolutely set on playing on the record, and that they desired a higher percentage of their own songs. Agreed, the band and their new producer were off to Oxfordshire and Chipping Norton Studios. In the first three-day session with Wainman they recorded one of his songs, "Give A Little Love," two Faulkner/Wood compositions, "It's for You" and "Maryanne," plus a cover of the old Frankie Valli and the Four Seasons number, "Bye Bye Baby." The decision to record the latter had come from a get-together with the band at Paton's house where they were all encouraged to bring in copies of 45's they thought they could cover. "Bye Bye Baby," which had been featured in the Rollers' old stage act, was a unanimous choice. A great one, according to Wainman: "I was so relieved when I first heard 'Bye Bye Baby,' 'cause I knew that'd be a hit".

Immediately following the sessions, the Rollers were presented with the Carl Alan award for "Group of the Year" for 1974. The presentation took place at the Lyceum Theater, and the band was given the royal treatment with a face-to-face meeting with Princess Ann at the ceremony. Tam collected on a side bet that the Rollers would be asked for their autograph at the formal event (they signed all night long). Then it was a quick holiday for Paton, Woody, Eric, and Derek at a health farm in Hampshire. When they emerged from their secluded hideaway and turned on the radio, they found out that Wainman's earlier prediction was coming true. "Bye Bye Baby" was an unstoppable smash. No matter which pop station you turned to, it was on.

And, although they had had hits before, this one felt different. It felt like a number one. It didn't take long. The record debuted at number eight on the chart, it moved to number two in its second week, and hit the top spot by the end of the third—a position it would remain in for the next six weeks, selling upwards of 70,000 units per day at its peak. Four of those weeks were allotted for the Rollers back at Chipping Norton to record the rest of their second album, *Once Upon A Star*.

With the phenomenon of having a number-one single bringing on all types of requisite appearances and interviews, and the band having to stop recording to film sequences for their new television series, it's a wonder they were able to actually finish *Once Upon A Star*, but, somehow, Wainman was able to deal with the interruptions and keep the band focused on the task at hand. It's an achievement he attributes partly to a lack of interference from the usually meddlesome Paton. "To be honest, I didn't see very much of Tam. He would just turn up for the odd session. When the boys were in the studio, I was completely responsible for them. It was fantastic, great fun. I booked a studio I didn't think anyone would ever find us at, and fans invaded it. You'd never seen anything like it. But that was a sign of the times, and it was just quite incredible. They were just great fun sessions. We worked very hard, we would be there until four or five o'clock in the morning, crash out in the hotel, and go back again … just work really, *really* hard, and we made an album in a month. The record company couldn't believe that I brought the record in on time and under-budget." More amazing still when you figure that with *Rollin'* the band had actually played most of the numbers through in their live set. *Once Upon A Star*, featuring seven new originals out of twelve songs that couldn't be rehearsed, afforded them no such luxury. The official breakdown of the album was seven for the band, three from Goodison/Wainman, and two remakes: "Bye Bye Baby" and another run through of "Keep on Dancing" with Les where Nobby used to be.

Getting to those numbers didn't happen without a bit of drama. At one point, David Walker—who managed Wainman—

told Bell/Arista that if "Phil doesn't get his five songs, he won't produce it." Coming on the heels of a number one, this was no idle threat.

Faulkner left the sessions immediately. Paton, feeling the glare from London, was ready to give in to Walker and Wainman's demands, even knowing it may have cost him his lead guitarist, until Barry Perkins stepped in to remind Tam that not only did Eric play, he was the principal songwriter. That meant his songs would be gone, as would any band publishing money through Bay City Music, a company that had as two of its board members a certain Mr. Paton and Mr. Perkins. Five days later, after dozens of phone calls between the parties, all was right in the world. The compromise had been achieved with no lasting hard feelings. Faulkner actually took the time to write a song about the ordeal that would later become one of the band's biggest hits, called "Money Honey."

Sometimes lost in the shuffle of dates and facts are the inner feelings of the group members themselves who, it should be noted, had held up well through the entire blur of activity. With life turning into one continuous cycle of hotel rooms and limousines, the Bay City Rollers became more and more introspective and less involved with one another—and when they were together, the occasional squabbles had grown more and more frequent. This "non-communication" was a byproduct of spending so many hours together; they had become hardened. They were there for each other in a working sense, but they were hardly the brothers they might have been had Tam not worked them into the ground. Especially sullen were the founding Longmuirs. Alan, already feeling old at twenty-seven, had dropped occasional hints about leaving, and Derek, unable to commit time to a friend who desired a deeper, more meaningful relationship, expressed a desire to, "Just get away, cause we're missing so much." Wood commented on the underlying tension brought on by the workload: "Everyone was living each day very frustrated. It was impossible to even take a holiday, let alone sit and talk." Or, as Faulkner put it, "Fucking down is what I was."

But, in truth, there wasn't even time to be depressed. In an attempt to be "normal" and provide an escape, Eric and Woody purchased a farm together near the Edinburgh airport, with the idea that they would both live there and eventually convert it into a recording studio. It wasn't long before word got out that the Rollers had invested in real estate, and a conservative guess on the number of break-ins by fans was placed at ten, compounded by a fire that eventually gutted most of the place. Faulkner got a flat in London—not that he'd ever have time to be there either.

The Bay City Rollers' Granada television series, *Shang A Lang*, made its debut on April Fool's Day, 1975. The weekly series featured the band cavorting *Hard Day's Night*-style, performing their hits and introducing guest spots from artists like Gary Glitter, Showaddywaddy, and the Rubettes. Produced by Muriel Young, and eventually directed by Mike Mansfield, the show gave—if nothing else—regular exposure to the group on a weekly basis. For many British girls, it became required viewing as Tuesdays became "Roller Days" when they would rush home from school to see their idols in action.

The first six episodes featured a segment with legendary session musician "Big Jim" Sullivan, a burly guitarist whose resume includes over a thousand top-ten singles by artists as diverse as Frank Sinatra, Dusty Springfield, and Stevie Wonder. His work on *Shang A Lang* is a time that he does not look back on fondly. "I'd known Muriel Young for years. She had asked me if I wanted to do an educational show that would teach kids how to play the guitar. That was the original plan. Well, somehow that concept for my own show morphed into me appearing on *Shang A Lang* with the Rollers. I actually turned it down at first 'cause I'd been through the pop scene with Marty Wilde, Eddie Cochran, and Gene Vincent in the early days, and I just had no interest whatsoever in the teenyboppers. I'd seen what they could do. It was literally one massive seething scream from beginning to end. These girls would be shouting, screaming, and crying all at once. I just worried what would happen if they ever really got hold of me." Sullivan says being on the show was literally guilt by association for him. "They figured he's touched them, we need to touch him. One time at London airport there were like a thousand of these girls who spotted me and chased me all over the building. Thankfully, they let me run into the first class holding area, or I don't think I would have made it out alive. On one segment, I was supposed to play a classical solo, and they screamed the whole way through it. After that, I had to get off that show. I did the first six episodes and that was it. I just told Muriel I couldn't deal with that." As for his recollection of the Rollers, Sullivan adds, "They weren't all that developed as musicians, and I knew they used session guys on the albums, but it wasn't that strange for the time. They were better than some though—the Small Faces, for instance, couldn't play at all, not a bit." His time on *Shang A Lang* did give the music vet one memorable distinction. He laughs as he recalls, "I did a bit with the Bay City Rollers where I came on in a kilt. It was actually picked as the number seven worst television moment of all time in the U.K. years later. Something to be real proud of."

Mike Mansfield, who would go on to direct the pop music series *Supersonic*, weighed in on the criticism being leveled at the band: "They work very hard. They do play their own instruments. I know because I've heard their backing tracks and seen them record, and they play very, very well. They write very good songs, which they don't get enough credit for."

One thing they were consistently getting credit for was the fervor of the fans wherever they went. Rollermania became the target of many critics, saying it was a dangerous phenomenon that needed to be stopped before someone was seriously injured. The first sign that things had maybe gotten out of hand came at Mallory Race Park in the Midlands of England at a BBC Radio One road show broadcast. Titled "Fun Day," it was anything but.

Designed to be an appearance/interview and not a concert, it was arranged that the Rollers would arrive via helicopter. The location was a small wooden hut in the middle of an island surrounded by a half mile of water. The copter landed and deposited the boys, and within minutes the water was filled with desperate Rollers fans furiously swimming in their Roller gear toward the island. Once there, the band was trapped with no way to escape but in a powerboat—which of course caused the lake to be filled once again with swimming fans. The copter escorting the boat caused the wind to blow and made so many waves that it was called off. Eventually the band made it away—minus most of their clothes, which had been ripped off their bodies in the melee. Somehow, only forty or so girls needed attention at a local hospital. No one was seriously injured. Radio One presenter Emperor Rosko called it "… the most surreal thing I've ever seen in my life. Like something straight out of a monster movie."

With *Once Upon a Star* selling faster than even *Rollin'* had, the group began its second tour of the U.K., a thirty-date affair, on April 27 at the Apollo Theater in Glasgow. Living up to his promise, Tam Paton used Dave Eager as the compere' for the tour again; "I remember one show on the second tour when there was a reporter there from the *Melody Maker*…a more serious U.K. music weekly. It was to be expected that *Melody Maker* would not like the Rollers. I invited the reporter to come on stage with me. I introduced the Rollers on the second tour, after a music intro, by having a large banner unfolded—one of the fans had made it—saying 'We love the Rollers.' It was about ten feet by six feet. A spotlight came on it, then everything blacked out apart from the spotlight. Then the music started, the stage went to blackout, I ran off, and the lights came on with the Rollers. 'Well,' I said to the reporter, 'you bring on the banner. I will say…*Here is friend of the Rollers*…walk on with the banner…hand me a corner…wait for the spotlight…blackout and run off with me.' What he hadn't realized was if you watched me from the side of the stage… I used to swing and rock backwards and forwards on my feet. This was because when in the confines of the theatres the fans screamed. The sound hit you with such force that it physically knocked you backwards. I knew whenever I mentioned phrases like: 'I have just been talking to five guys backstage'…SCREAMS… 'Is there anybody here called…Eric, Derek, Woody?'…SCREAMS…before I had even finished, I needed to rock forwards before the screams hit me otherwise I would be blown backwards. Well the reporter came on stage...and when the screams hit him he totally froze! He literally didn't know what hit him. He was like a stunned baby...and I had to lead him onto the stage. He was totally dazed. He also realized though from his experience that the Rollers, after the first few notes, could not really hear what they were playing. The fact that they produced any sort of cohesive musical output was a measure of their skill...as they couldn't hear anything they were playing. There was no 'in ear' fill monitor back in the seventies. One had to be there to appreciate that any volume of sound produced from the stage, was equally drowned out by the Rollers' fans."

The Glasgow concert was an important show for many reasons, the biggest being the attendance of an advance contingent of Americans, including public relations maven Carol Strauss-Klenfner. "My husband Michael was working for Clive Davis, who had left Columbia Records and was starting a new label called Arista. The Bell Records artists were all inherited for the new label, and it was up to Clive to decide which ones were going to make the transition. The Bay City Rollers were one of the few who did. My company, CJ Strauss Public Relations, was doing publicity for Bell, and I got a call saying, 'We want you to consider working with this new band.'"

A meeting was then arranged with Strauss-Klenfner and Rollers business manager Barry Perkins. "We had met at the Plaza Hotel in New York, and I remember it being the smallest hotel room I'd ever been in. It was like a broom closet. So, we moved our meeting to the hotel bar, and Barry presented these big black scrapbooks filled with clippings from the U.K. Every one was full of pictures of these thousands of girls, all dressed in plaid. Riots ... crying ... the whole Rollermania thing. Front-page stories about this hysteria they were causing. I had never heard of the Bay City Rollers or Rollermania, but you sure cannot deny what I saw. It was incredible." From there it was on to Glasgow for a look-see for Carol. "I agreed to take on the group, and Barry and Tam arranged through Arista for us to come to Scotland...Sid Bernstein, Danny Fields from '16' magazine, and

Lisa Robinson from *Hit Parader*. We went to Glasgow as one big U.S. contingency. We figured, hey let's go take a look. Well, then we got there and saw for ourselves. It was insane. I remember the constant screaming from the fans. At the theater and at the hotel—those kids were literally everywhere."

Fields was blown away. "They were a phenomenon. Everything you heard about the hysteria was true. It's the first and only time I've seen a rock band shut down an entire city. Glasgow is like five million people, and it was completely in a state of gridlock because of the Bay City Rollers."

Mike Klenfner, who was running the Arista promotion department, remembers his wife's return from Scotland: "Carol had seen them in Scotland. She said, 'Michael, this will blow your mind.' She brought back all these pictures of the mania, and I thought, 'Oh my God, does this look fun.' After going over and seeing them myself, I came back and told Clive that we needed to keep this act on Arista."

America was next on the horizon for the Bay City Rollers, but it was a journey that almost didn't happen.

SIX

David (Stein) and Goliath

In his mid-fifties, David Stein now runs a New York-based mail order music business. But in 1975, he was working with one of New York's most legendary figures. "I was working with Sid Bernstein—the man who brought the Beatles to Shea Stadium. We were working with Jerry Weintraub and his organization. At the time, they had the '3 D's,' as we called them: Diamond, Denver, and Dylan. Jerry was red hot. In fact, he had one of the best relationships of anybody with Elvis, to give you an idea of how big he was. Anyway, Sid and Jerry had a falling out over his position, title, or whatever at a Frank Sinatra event, and that was it. We left Jerry and set up shop on our own. We were actually working out of Sid's apartment on Park Avenue. Out of his den. No secretary, no real office. Sid was determined to make it on his own, and he was able to grab an act or two right away, like Melba Moore and the DJ Cousin Brucie. But, we weren't exactly rollin' in it. Thankfully, there was a guy named Joe Taub who had done real well for himself with the company ADP and the Sir Speedy copy center franchise operation. Well, he wanted to be in the music biz pretty bad, so he was paying Sid something like five grand a month to find the next big thing. Figuring that Sid had the magic, you know? Well, it had been a long time since the Rascals, and like ten years since the Beatles. So, there was a bit of pressure to deliver, but because of Joe Taub there was some money coming in."

According to Stein, what happened next was a simple case of history repeating itself. "The famous story is that back in 1963, Sid enrolled in some classes at the New School for Social Research in the Village. He attended a lecture by Dr. Max Lerner from the *New York Post*. Lerner told the class that if they really wanted to learn about democracy in America, that it would be a great idea to learn about other democracies by reading newspapers from those countries. So, Sid started reading the British papers and the music papers like *Melody Maker*, and that is how he was able to get the buzz on the Beatles way before anyone else. A transatlantic call to Brian Epstein, and the rest is music history."

Flash forward with Stein to 1975: "I'm doing the same thing, reading all the British papers and every day there would be another story about the mania that was being caused by the Bay City Rollers. They were all over the front pages. Just like the Beatles had been years before. And, just like the Beatles, nobody in America knew who the hell they were." It was then that Stein laid it on the line. "I told Sid, these guys are a phenomenon over there, and we should check it out for ourselves. I showed him the newspaper articles and explained how big they were in the U.K.. We talked about the hysterical reaction they were getting, all the merchandise they were selling, and all of that. So, Sid and I went and met with Clive Davis, who was about to launch his new label, Arista, which was Bell Records at the time. Clive came from Columbia, so he had this image of an older, more sophisticated thing. He had no interest in the Bay City Rollers at all. Sid couldn't take no for an answer, so he decided to reach out to Tam Paton—who was managing the Rollers—and just like with Epstein it was very encouraging. So, Sid came to me and said 'I'm gonna go over meet with Tam Paton and Barry Perkins and would you like me to step aside and let you take care of it since you found them?' Out of respect for Sid, I said no. So, he and Joe Taub went over to see the Rollers and meet with them in Paris. Well, a little time goes by, and I'm thinking, you know maybe I should step in. I will never forget it; I was at Danny Goldberg's office. Sid calls and I said, 'I've been thinking about what you said. I do want you to step aside and let me work with the Rollers.' Too late. He said, 'Sorry David, but I can't do that.' He had already signed a contract to represent the Rollers in America."

Stein was crushed. "Sid Bernstein was like a father and a brother to me. I felt so betrayed and hurt. He knew all the hard work I had put into researching the Bay City Rollers and how much time I spent in putting together a plan for them to come to the States. I even stood up in a meeting with Clive Davis—and believe me, nobody stands up to Clive—and told him that he was wrong about the Rollers. I said these guys are gonna happen, but you've got to listen through the ears of an eleven or thirteen-year-old girl. They were not capable of seeing the band like a teenager would. Eventually, he came around and saw the potential. After what happened with Sid that day, I totally lost faith in people, and it took a real long time to get over it. The truth of the matter is, if it wasn't for me, no one in America would have heard of the Bay City Rollers."

An early publicity still. Not an ounce of plaid in sight. (L-R) Eric Faulkner, Nobby Clark, Alan Longmuir, John Devine, and Derek Longmuir. CREDIT: The Nobby Clark Collection.

1972 (L-R) Derek, Eric (tank top), Alan, John, and Nobby. CREDIT: The Nobby Clark Collection.

On the verge of Rollermania, 1974. CREDIT: Starfile

The self described "King of Hits," Jonathan
King.

The Fab Five pose for their debut LP cover. (L-R) Wood, McKeown, The Longmuirs (seated) and Faulkner. CREDIT: David Golumb. Courtesy of Tam Paton.

Showing off custom made 'Rollergear,' 1975. CREDIT: Tam Paton Collection.

The Band and the braintrust. (L-R) Derek Longmuir, Sid Bernstein, Woody Wood, Tam Paton, Barry Perkins, (front row) Eric Faulkner, Alan Longmuir, Les McKeown. CREDIT: David Golumb. Courtesy of Tam Paton.

On the set of the Cosell show. Woody, Sid Bernstein, and Alan. CREDIT: David Golumb. Tam Paton Collection.

The omnipresent and all powerful, Clive Davis.

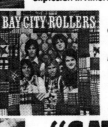

BCR 1975 CREDIT: Arista Records Publicity.

The band meets the U.S. press for the first time, on arrival in New York City 1975. CREDIT: Bob Gruen/Starfile

Rocking the sold out Santa Monica Civic Auditorium, 1977.

The BCR treatment for New York's Palladium
Theater, 1977. CREDIT: Bob Gruen/Starfile

Crouching Rollers, Hidden Paton. CREDIT: Jorgen
Angel www.angel.dk

A view from sidestage. CREDIT: Jorgen Angel www.angel.dk

Eric Faulkner giving 'big licks.' CREDIT: Jorgen Angel www.angel.dk

Derek Longmuir bringing the backbeat. CREDIT: Jorgen Angel www.angel.dk

Faulkner floored. CREDIT: Bob Gruen/Starfile

A bit of good advice for Eric from this group of London Rollermaniacs, 1975. CREDIT: Derek Ridgers

Another great escape, Los Angeles 1975. CREDIT: Bob Gruen/Starfile

Live at The Budokan, Japan 1976. CREDIT: Keystone Tokyo

Caught in the moment. CREDIT: Jorgen Angel www.angel.dk

Whooping it up for their heroes. CREDIT: Jorgen Angel www.angel.dk

Missed most of the show, but worth every second. CREDIT: Bob Gruen/ Starfile

Alan out and Ian in. Introducing the newest BCR, Ian Mitchell.
1976 CREDIT: Alan Ballard / Tam Paton Collection

Racking up the frequent flyer miles, 1976. CREDIT: Bob
Gruen/Starfile

1976: Woody on bass, Buffalo, NY.

Ian Mitchell CREDIT: Alan
Ballard/Tam Paton Collection

SEVEN

Bigger Than …
Well, at Least as Loud

Sid Bernstein agrees that Arista's Davis wanted no part of the Bay City Rollers. "I told Clive I was gonna go to Scotland to meet with the Rollers, and that I was thinking of bringing them to America. He didn't hesitate to tell me that I was out of my mind. He said he didn't think they played on their records and that I'd lose every bit of my credibility in the business." Bernstein was undeterred. "Of course, I didn't listen to him. I had nothing to lose, so I went over, saw it all happening, and signed them on the spot."

It didn't hurt the band's standing with Davis that his friend—and their original Bell producer—Jonathan King recommended that he stick with them. Over breakfast, Davis put it to King this way: "Jonathan, can this band happen in the U.S.?" King's answer was, "My head says no but my heart says yes." According to King, Davis pushed aside his eggs, sipped his coffee, and after a long time replied, "OK, I'll go with your heart."

In a May 18th press release, Sid Bernstein took up the gauntlet in his inimitable style, announcing to the world that he had indeed signed the BCR to an exclusive contract as their American representative, saying, "I am getting a flood of inquiries at my New York office about the Rollers. We can do the

Superdome in New Orleans and make $400,000 in one night, which would be a record. Word has gone out to young people, and they tell me tartan plaid is already the in-thing. The people of America are ready for the Rollers. They're looking for new heroes, and these boys could be just what they want."

You wouldn't know it by the reaction that had been garnered in the States from the first few singles released there. "Summerlove Sensation" and "Bye Bye Baby" had both been serviced to radio only early in the year and had been met with a complete lack of interest and zero airplay.

Meanwhile, Carol Strauss-Klenfner was using the time before their arrival to work on a unique way to break the band. "We sat down and came up with a plan to bring them over to America. The basic concept was something I called the 'Bay City Roller Bulletin': a simple card that fit into a number ten envelope. We used a 'tartan-ized' typeface and included on each was a Xerox copy of these news clippings that were in Barry's scrapbook. No explanation, no hard sell. We sent them out each week. Fifteen or twenty a week to the tastemakers in the industry: obviously the gossip columnists, trade press, and even to executives at other competing record companies. It was a great tool for word of mouth."

'*16*' magazine's Danny Fields had work to do too. "I came back from Scotland and had to convince our publisher at '*16*' that these guys were worth writing about. It was a much harder task than you would think with the reaction they were getting over there. But, he was one of those guys who don't know something's happening until it's happening. You know, they don't know you're famous until you're famous. The attraction was simple. Girls, lots of them, were screaming. If you're in my business at the time that is reason enough to be interested. Girls are screaming, you pay attention. I had been through it with David Cassidy, I saw the Beatles at Carnegie hall. It was the same thing. Tried and true hysteria."

Back in the U.K., with America still four months away, it was hysteria of a different sort that marred the end of what had been a wildly successful British tour. With a day off between dates in

Great Yarmouth and Bristol on May 29, Les McKeown decided to fly back home to Edinburgh for a twenty-four-hour break. The nineteen-year-old singer was driving with a girlfriend and his brother Hari in his Ford Mustang on the Corstorphine Road. Says McKeown, "I was driving at about forty miles per hour and this woman was standing at the side of the road obviously undecided about whether or not to cross. I blipped my horn, and it seemed that she had seen me and was going to wait, then she suddenly stepped out into the road. I swerved to avoid her, but I had no chance. I was sideways on when I hit her, and then I crashed through a brick wall." Euphemia Clunie, seventy-six, lay dead on the road.

Everyone in the Mustang was shaken, but fine. Predictably, the next day's headlines screamed:

BAY CITY ROLLER DEATH CRASH!

The news of Clunie's death shook McKeown badly. "Seeing somebody lying dead in the street is something you never get over." A court date was set for November. Les was charged with vehicular manslaughter. In the meantime, says McKeown, "I had to rejoin the tour the very next day for a gig in Oxford. It was during that concert that I got involved in the punch-up with a photographer that led to another court appearance and a fine of £1,200 for assault." Understandably, the stress was getting to him. "I just wasn't in control of myself. Can you imagine what it was like to be on stage with all these chicks screaming at you when only the day before you've knocked somebody over and killed them? My head was buzzing, and I was thinking to myself, 'What the hell am I doing here?' It was the same with the next gig we did, but that time I just couldn't take it any more, and I broke down in tears and had to leave the stage. I felt very strongly that those concerts should have been canceled in view of my accident, but Tam insisted that we couldn't call them off at such a late hour."

And it was indeed business as usual for Paton and the band as they continued to plow forward, working at the customary breakneck pace. In the days following the end of the tour, it was off to Germany to do television, back to London to accept *The Sun's* "Top Pop" award at the Hilton, and then Manchester and the Granada TV studios for more *Shang A Lang* tapings. That is where tragedy struck again.

On June 14, 1975, Cliff Richard was the Bay City Rollers' musical guest on *Shang A Lang*. As he left the studios to go back to his hotel, the fans, not knowing who was inside the van that was pulling away, assumed incorrectly that it was the Rollers and stormed the vehicle. In the ensuing rush to restore order, an off-duty Manchester policeman who was moonlighting doing security detail suffered a massive heart attack and was dead on arrival at the hospital. Once again, bad news seemed to be everywhere the Rollers were. And, once again, the group was given no time to deal with it. They were back in front of the cameras within hours of the officer's death. Cliff Richard expressed his condolences to the family of the officer and wished the Rollers well in the future, saying, "I hope they get through this period of fan mania and keep their following so that audiences start listening to their music. It's very nice when that happens."

While Brits endured a sweltering heat wave in the summer months of 1975, the Rollers were seemingly even hotter. On July 7th, the band's next single, "Give a Little Love," was released, and it took up right where "Bye Bye Baby" had left off, entering the chart at number seven. It was number one by the end of the week and stayed there for an entire month.

As the band began recording demos for their next album, Tam Paton was busy burning up the phone lines between Edinburgh and Sid Bernstein's office in New York. Plans continued to be formulated for their trip abroad, which was now scheduled to take place in September. Paton was thinking globally as he began to pencil in trips for the band to Norway, Finland, Denmark, Switzerland, Australia, and New Zealand— all set to take place before year's end. But it all hinged on America—where David Stein was very busy.

"We did a lot of work getting America ready for the Rollers," Stein says. "Tony Kornheiser—who is now a big sports guy on

ESPN—wrote a very early story that ran in *Newsday* for us. Through my contacts I was able to get a video clip of the band on the old kids show *Wonderama* with Bob McCallister. So that was their first TV exposure in August." They were looking for something bigger to use as a stage for the band's U.S. introduction when it was announced that sportscaster Howard Cosell was getting his own ABC variety series.

Saturday Night Live with Howard Cosell would debut in September. The timing and the format were eerily similar to another British band's American coming-out party—a fact that didn't go unnoticed by Faulkner at the time. "Cosell is doing something like the old *Ed Sullivan Show*. I remember what that did for the Beatles, so we're hoping it will be the same for us." Stein and his boss had the same aspirations. "I called Howard Cosell personally," says Bernstein. "I said, 'Howard, I just came back from Scotland where I saw and signed a great new act. I think they could put your show on the map.'" Cosell referred Bernstein to the producer of the show, comedian Alan King. King agreed to meet with Sid and David at the office of ABC's Roone Arledge. "I passed out pictures of the Roller crowds to the two of them and said look, this ain't the Beatles, but the reaction is the same. I said if you put these guys on your show you'll have a completely out-of-control scene like none since the Beatles." Sid's sales pitch worked, and King and Arledge agreed that they would take the band.

For David Stein, it was the news he had been waiting for. "We finalized the deal with ABC for the Cosell show. We'd get custom video from a show in London and air that the first week, followed by a real live performance at the Ed Sullivan Theater two weeks later."

ABC executives were also crossing their fingers for success. Stein recalls, "The network was full of high hopes for that show, 'cause Cosell had this amazing 'Q' (identifiable) rating. It was like number three behind Gerald Ford and Muhammad Ali. The part they hadn't figured out is that his number was so high because everybody hated him so much."

Even with no television or a U.S. single release, the group was developing a small buzz with some New York-area teenagers. Stein continues, "There was an early group of girls who knew who they were because they were reading all the British mags and newspapers on my urging. They kinda looked to me as a visionary, and they were pretty hip. The Rollers turned them on so they turned their friends on." Stein was confident that the band's success would translate across the Atlantic. "I knew that they would do well here. It was clear that they would be a phenomenon, and—I stand by this today—they were the first real worldwide pop music phenomenon since the Beatles, and there have only been one or two since."

In Oxfodrshire, the group and Phil Wainman continued working on tracks for what was to be their next album, *Wouldn't You Like It*. It would serve as a creative turning point for the band; every song on the album would be penned by Faulkner and Wood. One track from the sessions that would not be included on the album was instead released as their next single, the Perkins/Goldberg/Paton-inspired "Money Honey." The song featured this bit of Faulkner vitriol: *Money honey you ain't got no respect, snide like a fox yeah just to see what you can get*. It was a classic line that ended up as one of the all time most "misheard" lyrics. Around the world, many were singing "Down by the horseshed," "Down by the forkshed," or with *Welcome Back Kotter* devotees, "Down by the Horshack ... just to see what you can get."

Truth was, as songwriters, Eric and Woody were spreading their wings. Phil Wainman says, "I think they did improve as songwriters. They obviously wanted to do their own thing; they wanted to make their stamp on their music with their own material. They wanted to become known as another Lennon and McCartney."

David Stein concurs, "I was extremely impressed by what Eric and Woody were writing, and if I'd been able to continue working with them, I would have encouraged their development as songwriters. They were every bit on par with John and Paul at the same stage in their writing career. You know, a year or so in.

Listen to 'Marlina' or 'Maybe I'm a Fool to Love You' now and see if you don't agree. Those were good songs. 'La Belle Jeane' reminds you of 'Michelle' by the Beatles. The difference is, the Rollers were not allowed to get better at their craft. They stagnated from there, which, is a real shame. In my way of thinking, the Rollers could have been that generation's Beatles and the Sex Pistols could have been the Stones, but it didn't work out that way."

The sessions for the album continued throughout the month. By the end, producer Wainman had had enough. "When I got there, the boys had already decided they weren't gonna cut the songs that Clive Davis wanted, and that they had written some songs themselves, and these were the songs that they were gonna record. So I said, 'Look, I don't wanna get involved in the politics of this, and I think I'm going to leave you to it'—and I just left them to it. But that's when Clive Davis came over and said, 'We still want you to produce the band, you make a great team and everything.' But there were just too many influences there, too many cooks and no one's running the show, everyone's trying to influence it. I didn't wanna get involved in the politics of it, so I just walked away from it." With Wainman's abrupt departure, musical director Colin Frechter became the go-to guy for the rest of the sessions. Frechter, the one-time producer for the Troggs, had been involved since "Bye Bye Baby" and had earned the respect of the group members by staying down on the studio floor with the band throughout, while Wainman sat in the upper-level control booth.

He remembers the day that the Rollers became his: "Phil picked me up at my place and was grumpy about something. A few hours later, at the studio, I said, 'Where's Phil?' and the response was 'He's gone, it's over.' There had been some sort of row over the songs which I didn't hear. I got a call from his partner David Walker, who said, 'You'd better stay there and help them. Don't let the office down.' So, I went ahead with the sessions. Then I get an angry call from Phil saying 'Why did you jump in?' I told him that the guys had asked me to and that I'd said no, but then David asked and I said yes. It was a tough spot to be in, but the result was 'Rock 'n' Roll Love Letter,' which Clive had picked for them to cover, and I think it came out quite nice in spite of it all. In fact, Clive loved it. He called me at home to ask that I bring the vocals up a bit, but that was the extent of the remix." Faulkner was very pleased with that recording, saying later, "That was one of the best records we made, really, and I think it was because it was done with Colin."

As Sid Bernstein continued to hype the impending arrival of "the next Beatles," Clive Davis interceded and switched the Rollers' first commercial U.S. single release from the U.K. hit "Give a Little Love" to the more up-tempo "Saturday Night." With a release date set for September 15th, Alan, Eric, Woody, and Tam made a quick promotional run to Adelaide, Brisbane, and Sydney while Leslie, still reeling from the emotional aftermath of his accident, was given permission—as was Derek—to return to Edinburgh for a rest. When they returned, the band convened at London Weekend television studios on September 20th to perform a special lip-sync "concert," part of which ("Saturday Night") would be carried live via satellite on the Cosell show. The show in its entirety would be broadcast as a "Night Flight" special at a later date. The audience of 600 Rollermaniacs was small by concert standards but made for an extremely packed TV studio. Egged on by the provocative antics of Wood, Faulkne,r and McKeown, the girls got progressively out of hand as the night wore on. With security doing everything they could to hold them back, madness ensued. It was just the kind of hysteria that Paton and *Shang A Lang* director Mike Mansfield had hoped for—and then some. By concert's end, Eric's pants had been ripped away, and Woody was knocked unconscious for over ten minutes by a "well meaning" fan. An audience estimated at twenty-five million Americans witnessed the orchestrated mayhem. They were about to get a much closer look. On September 30, the boys boarded their 747 at Heathrow airport in front of a few thousand well-wishers. Next stop...New York City.

As the Rollers set foot on American soil for the first time, they were greeted by a couple hundred "in the know" American fans, including a few who had gotten "help" with their transportation to JFK Airport from Sid Bernstein. Carol Strauss-Klenfner remembers that day: "There was a real scene at the airport. So many people. I actually got shoved onto one of those baggage carousel things that go round and round and took a little ride with my legs up in the air. Quite a sight, I'm sure. But it was about what we had expected. Lots of cameras, a definite buzz." She was impressed with the band's work ethic and was amazed by how small they were. "They were so little physically. Just tiny guys. My initial impression of the Bay City Rollers is that they were so sweet, excited, young, and fresh. They were ready to work long and hard to get to where they needed to be. They had a natural charm, and I remember thinking that they were very green about the business. At least on the surface." And work they did. A peek at the band's itinerary for their five days in the USA gives you an idea of just how hard:

Tuesday, September 30

2 P.M.	Arrive at JFK airport from London (nine-hour flight). Clear customs.
4 P.M.	Check in Westbury Hotel. Press Conference.
5 P.M.	Visit from Howard Cosell
6 P.M.	Dinner and coctail party at Maxwell's Plum
8 P.M.	Gather to watch Ali/Frazier "Thrilla in Manila" fight on HBO.
12 A.M.	White Castle hamburgers
1 A.M.	Tour of Harlem and Apollo Theater
3 A.M.	Bed

Wednesday, October 1

7 A.M.	Visit the first of ten radio stations
1 P.M.	Lunch at Arista Records
3 P.M.	Photo shoot at Rockefeller Center
6 P.M.	Dinner with radio station winners
9 P.M.	ABC party
12 A.M.	Bed

Thursday, October 2 *(technically a day off)*

11 A.M.	Interviews with magazines and newspapers at the hotel
1 P.M.	Sightseeing, including Empire State Building
6 P.M.	Dinner with Arista
12 A.M.	Bed

Friday, October 3

6 A.M.	More radio visits (three stations).
11 A.M.	Photo shoot/shopping at "Manny's" music store.
1 P.M.	Jewelry factory tour/shopping
3 P.M.	Rehearsal for *Howard Cosell Show*
6 p.m.	Dinner with public relations crew

Saturday October 4

Noon	Lunch and photo shoot at Nathan's Famous Hot Dogs
3 P.M.	Dress rehearsal
5 P.M.	Helicopter to Staten Island Bloomingdale's for autograph session
7 P.M.	Police escort to Ed Sullivan Theater. *Howard Cosell Show.*
11 P.M.	Flight to Bermuda

Their time in America was well spent, the whirlwind of interviews and the Cosell appearance giving the "Saturday Night" single a nice kickoff. But an immediate speed bump for the first single was the "bigger than the Beatles" propaganda that

Sid Bernstein was spewing. Quite a few radio programmers were resistant at first because of the perceived hype.

Carol Strauss-Klenfner says, "Sid made the mistake of using the term 'the next Beatles' in a story that the *New York Times* ran. That was very unfair to the band. There is no such thing as the next Beatles or the next Elvis. They were a fun teen-oriented pop group. Why didn't this generation deserve its own teen idol group? Instead of comparing it to something else, let it be what it is. It was very frustrating."

Her husband, Arista's Mike Klenfner, didn't appreciate the constant comparisons either. "Sid Bernstein had made the ridiculous statement that the Bay City Rollers were going to be bigger than the Beatles. Tom Parker never said that Elvis would be bigger than Sinatra. Brian Epstein never made the claim that the Beatles would be bigger than Elvis. On the one side, Sid's statement brought a lot of notoriety—but not the good kind. I mean, say that you'll be big. Don't say bigger. That's called hype. He also claimed early on that they could sell out Shea Stadium, which was ridiculous. I mean, the Fox Theater in Atlanta yes, the Beacon sure, Steel Pier in Atlantic City, no problem…but Shea Stadium? C'mon!"

Even the band members themselves grew to resent it. Woody Wood later said, "The reaction we got was definitely similar to what the Beatles had. But comparing a band to the Beatles really turns people off. Nobody can write or sing like the Beatles did. If somebody in the crowd screams, immediately you're being compared to the Beatles. It turned people off, and that's understandable. You have to be yourselves and have your own thing to offer. I place a lot of it on Sid Bernstein. He was telling people we'd fill Shea Stadium! I mean it was total bullshit. Sid is a great person, one of the nicest people I've met in the business, but he really was guilty of over-selling the band. Too much hype."

Klenfner continues, "It really made our job a lot harder, Sid making that 'bigger than the Beatles' statement. That put such a bad taste in the mouth of the rock press from the very beginning. They would literally hate 'em without even hearin' 'em. It's like 'don't tell me that something's going to be as big as something I have loved and cherished for years … you know, fuck you!"

One person who wasn't bothered at all by the comparison was former Beatle George Harrison, who, in the fall of '75 said, "In some ways, I feel out of touch. To tell you the truth, I've still never even heard the Bay City Rollers."

The determination of the Arista staff to "bring it home" started at the top with Davis making it clear to them all that "Saturday Night" was an important record. "Clive was bound and determined to start Arista with some hits," says Klenfner. "Barry (Manilow) and Melissa (Manchester) had gotten us close with a couple of songs, but he really wanted a number one. We loved it because it wasn't the 5th Dimension or Tony Orlando. No offense to them, but who gives a shit? This was young and new. I remember thinking this will be fun. A lot of fun."

Carol Strauss-Klenfner admits that, for her publicity firm, CJ Strauss, it was a nerve-wracking time. "Promoting a band is like building a house of cards. You have to be very careful because one strong wind and the whole thing will blow down. We had Lisa writing the band up in *Hit Parader* and *Creem*, Danny and '16' were all over them, and as I recall, *Tiger Beat* in Los Angeles had a lot of early interest as well. Before their arrival, it was like waiting for a flame to build. Then we endured all the Sid backlash, and once they got a hit song it just took off from there."

Mike Klenfner attributes the song's eventual success to the leg work the band did during that first visit. "I literally took them everywhere. Of course all the big radio stations, WFIL in Philly, WRKO in Boston. We arranged a dinner with the Ramones 'cause they all were big Rollers fans. I took 'em to the 'Airplane' house to meet the Jefferson Airplane and their manager, Bill Thompson. Needless to say, that was crazy and a little surreal." More important, says Klenfner, was the undeniable fact that the song was a hit. "Dave Sholin, who was the Music Director at KFRC in San Francisco, told me what I'll never forget as the turning point of the 'Saturday Night' campaign…he said, 'Mike, this thing is exploding on its own without any airplay. I'd be stupid to not give our audience what they want. We're going to start playing this record.' It was a great song that just leapt off the radio."

Says Sholin, "'Saturday Night' was a smash. As we say in radio, 'on and gone,' meaning it was a hit from the start. Within two days it was our most requested song, and, in relation to everything else, it wasn't even close. In those days we didn't have computers, so all the requests were tallied by hand. I remember seeing the request sheets, pages and pages of sheets filled with these little pencil tally marks. The second most requested song for those first few weeks would have like thirty or so requests and 'Saturday Night' would have hundreds. It was mostly young girls, but when they speak, you listen."

Sholin's enthusiasm for the record was shared by his peers across the country as, slowly but surely, the disc started to make an impact on U.S. top-forty playlists. It debuted inside Billboard's top-forty chart on November 8th. New York's WABC debuted the record at number twenty-five on the 18th. WQXI Atlanta and WLS Chicago followed soon after. By the end of December it was indeed Arista's first ever number one single, certified gold on December 16th. The man who selected it, Clive Davis, says there's a reason why: "It was such an anthem. Purely, and simply, a hit record."

The Rollers weren't done with their 1975 assault on the planet. The successful American visit was followed by concerts in Norway, Finland, Denmark, Sweden, and Switzerland. And it was on that tour that Les McKeown was almost caught red-handed in his effort to be red-blooded. He recalls, "It was four o'clock in the morning, and a friend and I were having a great time with two Swedish girls in my Stockholm hotel room. Suddenly there was a knock on the door. Instant panic! We knew it must be Tam Paton checking up to make sure we weren't doing exactly what we were doing. We hurriedly bundled the girls out on the fire escape in the scantiest of underwear before we let him in and then pretended that we had just been chatting. For once Tam seemed satisfied that we had been behaving our-selves, which was amazing since, as I knew from past experience, he could normally pick up the scent of a girl's perfume in the air from the other end of the corridor! To our horror, he settled down for a chat. That was the usual excuse for his check-up visits to hotel rooms at odd hours. My mate and I put on a great show of yawning and saying how tired we were, but he stayed for more than half an hour. By the time the coast was clear and we were able to let the girls back in, they were literally blue with cold. I was involved in a continual game of cat-and-mouse with Tam over girls. As far as he was concerned, going out with a girl was the worst sin you could commit as a Bay City Roller. He had this bee in his bonnet about the group's image; he was convinced that we must appear to be unattainable and untouchable."

After a short break back home, it was off to Australia, where the band played nine shows in eleven days. The pace and heat caught up to Wood, who collapsed onstage in Melbourne. The guitarist was hospitalized for dehydration and exhaustion, missing the Canberra, Sydney, Brisbane, and Newcastle performances all together.

With the band returning home on December 10, Les McKeown once again dealt with controversy as he was awakened at his Edinburgh home the next morning by Lothian and Borders police wanting to know if the singer owned a gun. It seems a fifteen-year-old fan who had been outside the home had been taken to the hospital the night before after having been shot in the head with an air rifle pellet. McKeown had hosted a party that night but claimed ignorance of the matter. "The first thing I knew about the incident was when the police arrived at the front door the next morning and asked if I owned an air rifle. I couldn't understand what it was all about and straight away told them, 'Sure I do—it's right here by the door where I always keep it.' They then announced that someone had been shot and they needed to take the gun away as evidence. The next thing I knew they were charging me. I thought at first a neighbor must have done it. It was some time before this guy who was staying with me came forward and admitted it was him. I said, "In that case you'd better get down to my lawyer quick, because otherwise I'm going to get done for it." Afterwards I felt a bit sorry for the guy; after all, a lot of people wouldn't have had the guts to own up when somebody else was set up to take the rap. So, we gave him a minor job in the Rollers organization. It was a gesture of forgiveness that backfired on me in a way, because there were plenty of people who put two and two together and made five and wrongly assumed that the job was his reward for providing a false confession and cooperating with the officials."

For the British press, it was an opportunity to revisit the "Bay City bad boy" theme of the articles that had been written in the wake of the auto accident a few months prior. The public relations nightmare was short-lived; the previous vehicular manslaughter charge was reduced to reckless driving, resulting in a fine and the one-year suspension of McKeown's driver's license. As the legions of Les fans breathed a collective sigh of relief, the Rollers released their third U.K. album, *Wouldn't You Like It.* It entered the British charts on December 13th and would eventually end up at number three. The group's self-titled U.S. debut album, *Bay City Rollers*—a mixture of tracks from the first two albums plus "Give A Little Love" and "Saturday Night"—was released at the same time.

The band finished up 1975 with two shows in Belfast, Northern Ireland. Just before the flight, Alan Longmuir was bitten on the backside by a horse he was riding. Ironically, he was about to be bitten even harder. Unbeknownst to the eldest founding Roller, his days in the band were numbered, and his eventual replacement was ten years younger and playing rhythm guitar for the Irish opening act.

Ian Kevin Mitchell (b. 8/22/58) grew up in Downpatrick, Northern Ireland, and formed his first group, Albatross, with classmates at the age of thirteen. Albatross became Bang, and began to develop a local following. Mitchell recalls, "Cecil Thompson was the hottest agent in Ireland at the time, and he booked all the big shows. He started using us to open for bands that were in the charts. He convinced a guy called Morris Cassidy to let us open for the Rollers when they came to Ulster Hall in Belfast. So, we did that for like 1,800 people. The hits at that point were 'Remember,' 'Shang A Lang,' and 'Summerlove Sensation.' We opened for 'em and did every one of those songs in our set. Needless to say, Morris wasn't real happy about that, but the Rollers didn't mind. In fact, Tam thought it was great. We swapped numbers, and I even went so far as to ask him if we could get an acetate of their next single, in advance, so we could learn it right away. He thought that was a wonderful idea."

The similarities in the bands and their mostly female followings weren't lost on Thompson, who suggested that the group make the connection even more obvious. "Cecil's idea," says Mitchell, "was that since we were basically Bay City Rollers clones, we should change our name to something similar. So we became the Young City Stars and started packin' 'em in—big crowds of Rollers fans who figured we were the next best thing. We just did the circuit and wore the tartan and everything. About the time that the Rollers had gone to number one with 'Bye Bye Baby,' it was announced that they were coming back, this time to the Belfast Odeon. Morris Cassidy allowed us to support them again but warned us very sternly to behave. He said, 'Look guys, no leaning, and no inciting. Just play.' Well, the night comes, we're opening for the Rollers again, and if you thought Morris had been upset before, this time he went through the roof. See, we had these little four-by-six postcards made up with our picture and 'Young City Stars' on them. We waited till our last number and then threw them out into the crowd. It was a fuckin' riot in front of the stage. The girls were goin' crazy to get these cards. Morris was pissed. Thankfully, Tam stepped in and said, 'Hey, they're just kids. Leave 'em alone.' He was laughing about it and just figured that it would be that much easier for the Rollers to go over now that we'd wound up the girls so much."

Paton and Eric Faulkner also made note of the sixteen-year-old Mitchell as a potential replacement for Alan Longmuir, who was now very serious about a girl and becoming less enchanted with the day-to-day life of a Roller. Paton explains, "Alan had developed a relationship with a girl and was making it very clear that he was unhappy. Eric was also sensing that, and he complained to me that it was getting more difficult to get the work done. Alan was literally flying in to lay down his parts during the last record. At that time, his horse and girlfriend were more important. He just wanted more time to himself. He had a love-ly place up North, and I think, also, he thought he was a million-aire. Which of course, he wasn't."

Longmuir concurred with that description of his mindset at the time: "Sometimes I wish it would all just stop, so I could go out my own front door, walk down the street to look at the shops, then come home quietly and watch telly like anybody else." But besides the desire to be free, Alan was also bothered by the more frequent infighting within the group ranks, explaining, "We'd go onstage and smile all the way, then come back off and start arguing again. That's when it was getting to me. I said, 'I've had enough of this.'" It would take another few months to give him his desired emancipation, but the die had been cast and preparations had begun to ease young Ian Mitchell in and Longmuir out in the coming New Year.

EIGHT

Out With the Old, In With the 'Ludes'

Now that the band had their American breakthrough hit, the mission at hand for all involved was to keep them there. Strauss-Klenfner credits Tam Paton for being very clear about the image he wanted to project. "We were made aware that he had rules regarding smoking, drinking, and especially girlfriends. You were not to be photographed with a girlfriend. It was extremely important to preserve the illusion of availability to the female fans, all of whom needed to believe that Les or Woody could be their boyfriend. Tam was brilliant. He knew what the press wanted and had a very clear vision of that."

Woody agreed with that assessment of Paton. "Tam knew what he was doing—he was like a publicity machine. He had the 'gift of the gab' as we say in Scotland. He knew how to deal with people. He was good at keeping the band on the right track. If anybody started to slide off, he'd be right in there saying this is the way you should do it. He was quite strict in a lot of ways if you look at it from one side. But, looking back on it from an adult point of view, he was right on course, brilliant for the time."

Tam's "image first and always" directive was taken to heart by Arista's Klenfner. "We knew the only way to break them and keep them on top was through exposure and image. Especially

88

television. So obviously, the Cosell show was huge. The other thing was the teen magazines. Danny Fields of '16' deserves a lot of credit. He got it right from the beginning: access and, most importantly, for that audience, new photos. I mean a photo session with the band every twelve minutes. That was so key in keeping them fresh and exciting."

Fields says it was a symbiotic relationship for him. "I needed them to boost circulation. They needed me to sell records. I was given complete access to them for three years. On the road, at home, in the studio—anywhere. I was wined and dined; I'd hang with them in the hotel or whatever and come back with cute and kissy photos that are the lifeblood of a magazine like '16.' It was a relationship built on trust. They knew that I could blow it for them completely by telling secrets, but they trusted me to not do that. First of all, why would I want to wreck the fantasy of an eleven-year-old girl? They gave me their complete confidence, and I never exploited it. This band was fun and extremely professional."

Another person who was afforded 'all access' privileges was renowned rock photographer Bob Gruen, who remembers the band being a cash cow for him. "I made more money with them than I did with John and Yoko, or the Dolls, or anybody else I've worked with. I photographed a lot of bands back then, and when I was traveling in Europe or Japan I could go to the magazines and sell them two or three pictures each of Kiss, Debbie Harry, the Rolling Stones, maybe one or two of the Dolls, and thirty-seven or sixty-four of the Bay City Rollers. They might do a story on some of these bands, but they'd do a whole special issue on the Rollers. I was cleaning up. One of the first things I did with my Rollers money was buy a '54 Buick Special."

January 1976 found America beginning its celebration of its bicentennial birthday, and the Bay City Rollers were back for another whirlwind of publicity beginning on the 15th. To bolster the chart topping success of "Saturday Night," the Rollers visited New York, Atlanta, Philadelphia, Boston, and Detroit. The trip included meetings with Sid Bernstein and Clive Davis, in-store autograph sessions, the obligatory radio interviews, and even an audience with the mayor of Philly, who presented the band with keepsake miniature Liberty Bells.

Eric's "Money Honey" was released first in the U.K. in late November of '75, where it was business as usual; the song gave the Rollers their seventh consecutive top-five single, peaking at number three. It fared almost as well Stateside; it was released in early February and finished its run as the Rollers' sophomore U.S. offering at number nine on the Billboard singles chart. Quite a showing, but not good enough for manager Paton, who grumbled publicly that releasing Faulkner's song was a mistake and that the song wasn't as strong as their previous releases. That criticism stung Eric, who felt that he was continuing to lose the battle for control of the group's musical direction, and added to the funk he was in over the compromise of allowing the song's publishing to be split between the non-writing members of the group. Those issues, partnered with producer Wainman's departure and the mounting pressure being applied by Arista's Davis, wore on the guitarist, who was becoming more and more depressed as the weeks rolled by.

A Valentine's Day performance on Germany's "Bravo" television show was followed by an appearance in Italy at the San Remo song festival. Then, it was back to London for the Princess Alexandra Day Fund ceremony. The group had raised enough money in the preceding year's competition to purchase two handicapped buses and guide dogs. With the princess ill, Lady Norton accepted the check from the band in her place. At another London ceremony, the group was presented with *Music Week's* 1975 "Top Album Sales" award. Sensing the need to get a song on the British radio, music veteran Muff Winwood was called in to produce the band's next U.K.-only single, "Love Me Like I Love You," and its B-Side, "Mama Li." It was released on March 20 and would peak at number four a few weeks later.

At the same time, Ian Mitchell was the center of attention at Tam Paton's Preston Pans home. "Tam really wanted to build a band around me, so we took out an ad in *Melody Maker*. You know, 'Successful manager seeks... .' We got tons of responses, including a picture from Limahl, who went on to be in

Kajagoogoo. One day, Eric and Woody were at the house and Tam says, 'Ian, go with the guys to the studio and help them out.' So, off we go in the Range Rover to Castle Sound. I remember Eric saying, 'You know what's goin' on, right?' and I thought he meant that I knew Tam was trying to get me in a band so I said, 'Yeah, sure.' He wanted to know if I knew 'Money Honey' and a few others. And obviously, I did. No big deal, we go to the studio. Play and come home. Then Tam, Woody, and Eric go off down the hall and shut the door. I found out later that they had taped the session at the studio and were listening to the tape. I didn't know it, but I'd been auditioned for the Bay City Rollers."

The guitarist would figure it all out for sure a few weeks later. "This guy called Alan Wright who had been in Les's old band Threshold was at the house. He was a hairdresser and would cut the guys' hair. Tam says, 'I want you to get your hair cut.' I had real long rocker hair and was pretty proud of it so I said 'no way.' Then Tam says, 'You've got to keep up with the times.' I thought about it and figured, 'Well, he is just doing his job as a manager.' So I got a tuftie, the typical Roller cut, and it looked OK, although it was a little cold in the back where the hair used to be. Well then, one day soon after, Tam comes into the kitchen all white and wheezin', which is always a dead giveaway that he's nervous about something. Peter Powell, the Radio Luxembourg DJ was there, and Peter says, 'Can I congratulate him now?' And I say, 'For what?' Peter says, 'You're in the Rollers.' And I'm like, 'What?' and that was it."

It was April Fools' Day and the joke was on Alan Longmuir. He was out and Ian was in. Woody would pick up Longmuir's bass role and Mitchell would play rhythm guitar. In the end, Alan's burgeoning love life and lack of enthusiasm for the band was the culprit, not his birth certificate. Longmuir addressed the issues, saying, "I've learned it's not a question of age anymore because there are a lot of stars older than me and much bigger than I'll ever be. It's just a question of personality. I feel I'm disappointing a lot of fans that have followed me personally. But Ian is a lot younger than me, and he'll probably work a lot harder.

For me, it was great when it was all happening, but, I'm talking about eight years ago. I don't think the magic's there anymore."

In true Roller fashion, the transition was frantic. Mitchell remembers, "My first task was to find some Bay City Rollers clothes. I was like Jim Carrey in *The Grinch,* 'But, what will I wear?!' I asked for help, and Tam had me go through a box of 'Roller strollers' which were the pants that they sold to the fans through the fan club. Everything was too big, so I grabbed the smallest pair I could find and got out the sewing kit to take 'em in. I added a set of stars and stripes braces that I had, and that was my first set of Roller gear. The next day, the press arrived. Not just a couple of reporters mind you, but, literally van loads of press. And I'm like FFFFUUUUCCCKKK! The other guys in the band were there for a while, and I know them, but I don't *know* them, you know? We do a bunch of interviews and pictures, and then they were gone. Tam says, 'We're going to London tomorrow to shoot a video for "Love Me Like I Love You,"' which was the new single. It was a real concept number with Mike Mansfield from *Supersonic* directing ... a lot of dry ice and this big transition from Alan to me when the smoke goes away."

Most of the press accountings of the personnel move painted a positive picture of cooperation amongst the band members. Longmuir added to that spin, saying, "The other guys will stay my very best friends. And when they go in the studio, I'll still do some sessions for them, but I don't think I'll appear on the albums. It'll just be demo sessions because Ian will be playing in the Rollers. I've taught him a few things and Eric's showed him a lot about technique. So, I think he'll be a good replacement. I think Ian and I may share the bass playing on the next album. If the Rollers are ever stuck and they ask me to help them out, then I will. But I don't think that situation will ever arise."

Ian was still in the "pinch me, I'm dreaming" stage when he told *Melody Maker,* "You're bound to get real loyal Alan fans, but I don't think they'll upset me, and I hope to bring over more fans from the group I was in. The only real difference between what I was doing before and what I'll be doing now is that although we looked and acted like the Rollers, we didn't have the pressures they have, and we certainly didn't have the money. I can't really come to terms with it. I probably will over the next few weeks, but now it's a bit of a dream."

From London, the Rollers and their new charge headed off to Europe. Ian Mitchell recalls being thrown from the frying pan into the fire: "The first gig I did with the band was in Helsinki. I was shitting myself. It didn't help any that the guys from the band 'Mud' were on the show, and they kept winding me up. Askin' if I was nervous. It was all in fun. The one thing that stood out was this one chick that was holding up an 'Alan scarf' during the gig. I mean, there were plenty of 'Ian scarves,' but I couldn't quit lookin' at that one."

In the audience at that Helsinki show was Arista's Mike Klenfner and American record producer Jimmy Ienner. Handpicked by Clive Davis to produce the band's next album, Ienner brought an impressive resume to the table, having worked with the Raspberries and Three Dog Night among other '70s pop notables. Before committing to the project, he wanted the opportunity to see them play live. "Going in, I had one rule: they don't play, I don't produce. I had heard all the rumors that they didn't play on their own records and that some of their other records were mainly outside musicians. Arista was nervous. I flew to see them in concert and came away knowing they could do it. It was a feeling from what they were already doing and seeing the reaction of the audience that brought me to that conclusion. My attitude was I wanted it to be their record. I'd rather feel them doing something quirky than to make an album with no soul. The only way to get that is if they played. No problem." It was at that show that Ienner got his first in-person taste of Rollermania, "I remember a girl who must have been around fifteen or so had climbed up a flagpole. She got about half way up the thing trying to see the guys who were on the hotel balcony waving. And she lost her grip and fell all the way down into the small pool that surrounded it. She was screaming 'Woody, Woody, Woody' the whole way up and the whole way down. It was pretty comical to see and hear." There was more to come at the gig, says Ienner. "All these girls had been fainting. It was just a mob scene. There was this little lady working for the Helsinki Red Cross helping with medical attention. I happened to be standing there. She's like five feet one, 90 lbs. I'm six feet three, 210 lbs. She looks at me and yells, 'Are you with them?' I said yes and then she rears back with her little fist and smacked me straight in the jaw. I don't think she was dealing with it all very well." Also not dealing with it very well was Eric Faulkner, who was about to put a huge scare into everyone connected with the band.

The run through Finland, Amsterdam, and Germany concluded, and the group went on to Dublin, Ireland, to receive a TV award from *Starlight Magazine* and to tape the *Russell Harty Show* for ITV. It would serve as Ian Mitchell's first appearance in his native country as a Roller. A BBC documentary began taping on April 14. Says Mitchell, "It was just a crazy schedule. We flew in to London and stayed at the Holiday Inn. Then, we were set to catch a shuttle to Edinburgh in the morning. We had a BBC film crew from a show called *John Craven's News Round* traveling with us, and they were going to interview us at Tam's house the next day. Eric had taken something to help him sleep that night, and then, when we got to Tam's the next day, he took something else. I remember saying, 'Where's Eric?' and Tam said, 'Oh, he's being a pop star.' I knew the crew wanted him to be a part of the filming, so I walked down the corridor, opened up the door, and he's on the floor. I kicked him gently in the stomach to wake him up, and he just vomited. All of this greenish yellow stuff started coming out of his mouth with undigested capsules. I freaked and yelled for help. Tam's assistant Henry came in and said, 'He's OD'ed, call an ambulance.' So, we did. Tam's place was kind of out of the way, so I rode my motorbike down to the end of the lane so the ambulance would know where to turn. Of course, when I get down there, there's a big group of fans and they're all goin' crazy. I said, 'Look girls, now is not the time.' Sure enough, while I was dealing with them, the ambulance goes screaming right by. Eventually, they turn around and get Eric to the hospital. I know a lot of people think Tam called the papers before he called for an ambulance, but it's not true. He did call the ambulance first, and then he called Beth Coleman, our PR person, and I'm sure with us due to go to the States in three days, it was all about whether or not we should cancel the trip. Not about gettin' on the front page."

Tam Paton also denies the charge that he was more interested in headlines than Faulkner's health but cops to the fact that he realized that there was a publicity angle that needed to be worked. "I phoned for an ambulance first, but then right after that call I phoned the *Daily Express* and the *Daily Record* anonymously, saying, 'I hear that one of the Bay City Rollers had overdosed,' and that was it. The next day, we're on the front pages. Eric was in the Royal Infirmary and depressed. There were photographs of him coming out four days later going into hiding to recuperate."

The press accountings of the incident that ran the next day speculated that the Seconal and amphetamine overdose was not accidental and that the emotionally spent Faulkner had actually tried to kill himself. A notion the guitarist refutes today. "It was just a culmination from a couple of weeks of doing way too much. I wasn't sitting there thinking, 'I'm gonna take this bottle of Seconals and kill myself.' It was nothing like that. It was reported like that. Great! Another story. I just took too many. I only wanted to have a kip."

It was obvious to anyone that was near the band that the stress had gotten to Faulkner. Arista's Mike Klenfner felt the criticism that the twenty-one-year-old had endured was especially unfair. "I felt bad for Eric. He was very sensitive to the criticism they got. I also think he wanted to be respected for the music and his writing. A lot is made about Clive not letting them write or whatever. He didn't care about that. Clive Davis is smart. A hit is a hit to him. Whether it comes from an outside source or you wrote it yourself, it wouldn't have mattered as long as it was a hit. 'Money Honey' was a great song. Not as big as 'Saturday Night,' but it was a hit. They wrote it. As for them not playing on their records, I saw them play. I told Clive, 'Hey, they can fuckin' play, and they're pretty good.' The criticism was unfair, and then you get Eric taking uppers and downers over it. That's sad, and I felt bad for the kid."

On Sunday April 18, the band, minus Faulkner, boarded a plane in London to Los Angeles International Airport for the planned West Coast swing to promote the just released *Rock 'n' Roll Love Letter* album and single. The album was, for the most part, the U.S. version of *Wouldn't You Like It* with the same artwork. The only differences musically were "Money Honey" and the Colin Frechter-produced cover of Tim Moore's title track replacing the two songs that had already been used on their American debut disc. For California's BCR fans, it would be their first chance to see the band up close. Diane Stellman was one of the crowd of 300 or so Roller faithful at LAX that afternoon. "Tam came out first to tell us all to calm down. We didn't pay any attention 'cause we weren't even screaming. Unlike the East Coast girls, we were too cool for that business. My first reaction to seeing them was being amazed at how short and scrawny they all were. Ian was too close to us in age; he looked like he could have been someone's brother, just a baby. Plus, since he had replaced Alan, who we loved, he was like the fake Jan on *The Brady Bunch*. Derek looked old, Woody was reserved, so that left Les for us all to lust after, which we did."

The band checked in at the Beverly Hills Hotel after a quick run down Hollywood Boulevard. The next day it was a VIP tour of Disneyland with their guide, Mike Klenfner, who remembers, "We got the full-on Michael Jackson/superstar treatment. Private tour, no lines, and it was a blast. I've never seen a rock group get the reaction from the fans they got that day: instant recognition from everyone. Keep in mind, I've walked down the street with Mick Jagger and didn't get anywhere near that kind of reaction. I think we were all a bit traumatized by seeing Mickey and the other Disney characters with their heads off backstage. I still haven't quite gotten over that."

The next morning, local writers and photographers were invited to the band's hotel for a press conference and Q&A. McKeown spoke of the warm welcome given to the group on their first visit to the Golden State: "The reception here has been fantastic, it's more than we ever expected."

Derek Longmuir seemed equally surprised, saying, "A lot of people in the British press said we would never make it here because America is too sophisticated ... now we've had three hit singles and two hit albums here. I never thought it would happen so soon." After lunch, the Rollers were off to a Wherehouse Records store in Torrance for an autograph session—a crowd estimated at 1,200 was on hand for that. From there it was the NBC studios in Burbank to tape the *Midnight Special*. The group lip-synched "Money Honey" and "Rock 'n' Roll Love Letter" for the April 30 broadcast to be hosted by Ray Charles. A technicians' strike turned what should have been a two-hour job into a six-hour ordeal as technically inexperienced management struggled to get everything right for the taping.

A taping of *The Wolfman Jack Show* was first on the agenda for Wednesday the 21st, followed by another well attended "in-store," this time at the Sunset Boulevard Tower Records store. A visit to KHJ radio was the final piece of business for the day. San Francisco was next on the agenda, and the previous day's bedlam was recreated at the Columbus and Bay Tower store there. At the KFRC studios, Ian begrudgingly judged an on-air cookie contest. "I had never eaten a cookie in my life. I'd only had biscuits. I was totally grossed out by all the stuff in them. They said to vote for one, and I remember they all tasted the same. A lot of chocolate ... yecch! Funny thing is, now I can knock back a handful of 'Chips Ahoy' with the best of 'em." A swing by KYA was followed by sightseeing and shopping in Chinatown. The group then returned to L.A. and taped the first of what would be many appearances on the nationally syndicated *Merv Griffin Show*. When asked by the tartan-plaid-suit-wearing Griffin where Eric was, Les McKeown quipped that the guitarist had "the rockin' pneumonia and the boogie-woogie flu," a comment that got a laugh from the host and went straight over the heads of the studio audience and the young fans watching at home with their parents, unaware of the nasty truth.

The Rollers continued their promotional tour over the next few days with stops in Denver, Dallas, and St. Louis, where over 5,000 fans showed up for a retail appearance. They spent their final day of the trip in Miami on April 25, visiting top-forty station WHYI (Y100). Then, on April 26, the band arrived back at Heathrow airport, where they were met by, among others, their now well-rested and rehabbed lead guitarist. Eric Faulkner joined his bandmates for the flight to Berlin, Germany, where they received another award from *Bravo* magazine. Then, it was back to England for meetings and rehearsals with Jimmy Ienner, who recalls his musical mindset at the time: "I wasn't going to try and turn them into Pink Floyd. I just wanted to bring out their best. Optimize what they were. Rehearsals went very well. We had discussions about material. They hadn't written an abundance of new songs. We talked about direction with the concept being to nail the basics then take it and add a second or third tier. I call it putting all four legs on the table. Make it sturdy. And to not be afraid to take chances even if that meant that it could be a little outside of the expectations." He went on to explain how the decision to work with the band was made: "Clive Davis and I had a relationship that went back forever. He asked if I'd be interested. At that time, Eric Carmen had left the Raspberries and Capitol Records and was signed to Arista. So, as we were in-between that project and a Grand Funk live album that I was producing, I had a short window to do it. Keep in mind, I was also about to open my own label, Millennium Records, so it was a very busy time. But, the biggest factor was my own kids. My daughters loved the Bay City Rollers, so it was really done for them. I mean, I liked the boys, I liked their records. But, this was for my girls. I took a fee and set up a trust fund for my children with the money."

From May 1-10 the group rehearsed with Ienner in London. Ian Mitchell remembers the time as being an eye-opening experience for him. "It was a lot of fun, but hard work. I was starting to feel comfortable. Jimmy's a pro, and I learned a lot from him. For example, it was the first time that I'd seen a set of drums retuned for each track. It was a great experience. I learned a lot about song structure, arrangements and stuff. The best thing about Jimmy is he would take the time to explain things. You wouldn't just do it without knowing why. Jimmy Ienner was fine for the time. He's just a rock and roll guy. Tam was very nervous around him because he was really scared of anyone stealing us away. Just paranoid. Tam had way too much control. We all had our vision, and there would be the constant struggle for control—just a lot of bickering—and his presence was everywhere. It was like, give us a fuckin' break, man. *We're* the fuckin' band!"

The inner tension was obvious to Ienner. "It was tense for them internally. They had issues with Tam, and the splintering had begun. Leslie was already talking about going solo. They were all choosing sides to some degree."

Whether or not he was serious about leaving the band, McKeown expressed the opinion that the internal problems were amplified by Ian Mitchell's arrival, saying, "This stranger in the band is getting shoved in the front of pictures all the time. Weird shit like that." He lamented the change, saying that the family spirit that existed in the band before Longmuir's departure was gone. "The closeness we had, it wasn't there after Alan Longmuir was fired from the band."

Meanwhile, Eric Faulkner continued to express his displeasure with Clive Davis and the powers-that-be at Arista. He was upset over being overruled on his request that Colin Frechter be allowed to produce the album and miffed over the label's increasing desire to exercise creative control. After the experience of the completely group-penned *Wouldn't You Like It,* the label was insisting that the band enlist outside writers for their next project. Obviously, that meant less publishing income for Faulkner, and it was to change his entire outlook on the band, saying years later, "It's very hard to keep on writing songs when you know they're only going to use five. You get psychologically bogged down. In the back of your head you know they're only going to get put in a drawer. I mean, there were three guys writing in the band and we only had five songs per LP. That's one and a half songs each, one album a year. How can you build? You got a very negative attitude. Everyone in the band wanted to write songs but knew that they'd only use five at the most. They were just telling us to do that song, put that solo there. Any band could do that. It didn't mean anything. You do that for a few years and it starts to rub off on you. You start thinking like that, writing like that, playing like that. Eventually, we were just writing songs we knew would fit into the mold. The band was just sailing on the strength of what we'd been doing. We weren't even interested anymore."

The scoreboard would show that Davis got his way in regards to song selection. *Dedication* would ultimately only feature three Roller originals. The cover versions that would be recorded by the group included the Beach Boys' "Don't Worry Baby," Eric Carmen/the Raspberries' "Let's Pretend," a Russ Ballard composition called "Are You Cuckoo," a remake of the Dusty Springfield hit "I Only Want to Be With You," the Guy Fletcher-penned title track, and the seemingly autobiographical rocker "Yesterday's Hero" by the Australian songwriting duo George Vanda and John Paul Young.

According to Ian Mitchell, there was a master plan when it came to financial concerns. "Of course, I figured out the whole publishing angle later. I mean, it wasn't a coincidence that we did Eric Carmen's song 'Let's Pretend' and Jimmy just happened to have the publishing on it. Business is business." At the same time, he adds, the band was sometimes its own worst enemy in that regard. "They were actually offered 'Yesterday's Hero' like two years before for a 50/50 split and passed but ending up doin' it anyway. Woody and I wrote 'Write A Letter' with a little help from Leslie. Eric just wanted it all, and we didn't necessarily agree on everything in that regard."

Ienner says there was a simpler method to the madness. "Some of the songs, I had to talk them into. Really, they had no objections. The best way to get that balance and keep the peace comes from the old theory that comes from the days when you'd have nine or ten songs on an album. It's simply, three for me— meaning the producer/A&R guys—three for you—the band or artist—and three for them, meaning radio. It's a formula that works pretty well. I remember John Lennon putting it to use on

Walls and Bridges with 'Whatever Gets You Through the Night.' I'd be popping in and out of the room at the Record Plant and we knew that we needed one more for them, the radio guys. That last one was the big hit. With the Rollers, the obvious three for them were 'Dedication,' 'I Only Want to Be With You,' and 'Yesterday's Hero.' The rest took care of itself."

The divided group decided to get back together at the beginning of June and that the album would be recorded at KISS producer Bob Ezrin's new Soundstage Studio in Toronto, Canada, making it the first Rollers album recorded outside of the U.K. According to Sid Bernstein, the location was chosen to give the band's accountants a much-needed tax break. Not so, says Ienner: "We chose Toronto because I liked the idea of doing it there—added a little international flavor—and I had a lot of guys there that I could count on. Remember, David Clayton Thomas was from Canada, so we went back to the Blood, Sweat, and Tears days with a lot of these guys. Lighthouse guys, guitarists. Really it was just a good team in place, in Canada." It also would give the group the opportunity to be in close proximity of the U.S., where plans were underway to finally make their live concert debut.

After wrapping the quickie European tour, the Rollers touched down in Toronto on June 1st. The Canadian Rollermaniacs were in full force with over 5,000 greeting the band at the airport. That reception was an indicator of what was to come later in the month. The band began recording *Dedication* with Ienner behind the controls. "They were definitely still dealing with all the internal garbage. I had to record them in shifts for that reason. Once the basics were down, it was easier that way. You had a lot of division. I think Ian being new, was resented in a way by Les. Derek and Woody were the mellow guys. Eric was just plain irritated, but he came around eventually once we got down to it." Ienner recalls that the band had a great work ethic in the studio. "They worked very hard, knowing that we were limited in terms of time. They wanted it real bad and responded well to me pushing them to be great. All told, it was five or six weeks tops, not including rehearsals. Three weeks recording and another couple to mix."

According to Ienner, the sessions were memorable to those who worked at the studio because of the inherent mania that was always present wherever the Rollers were. "I remember the diversions we would have to always use at the studio, hotel, in the limos. We had to really beef up security. I mean there'd be these teen-aged girls with nothing on but raincoats. I probably spent my entire production fee on tips for the security guys. The girls were literally everywhere." Also present were some of music's biggest stars, and one that wanted to be there but couldn't. "John Lennon was actually planning to come and play on the record but never could get out of New York. He did attend the mixing sessions and got to hear it all there. Elton John came by but didn't play, and Rod Stewart was there too. The visit with Elton was fun. They had a nice mutual admiration thing from the U.K. The conversations were pretty surfacy. Typical musician stuff, but they had a lot of laughs with each other."

A break in the action came on June 26 when the group made their live concert debut in the States. Eight months past the Cosell show, and with Sid Bernstein's Shea Stadium promises now a faded memory, the group took the stage for a one-night-only performance to the strains of Elgar's "Pomp and Circumstance March Number Two" at Atlantic City, New Jersey's Steel Pier Music Hall. The forty-five minute set was later called "insipid and uninspired" by *Rolling Stone*. It didn't seem that way to the sold-out crowd of 2,000-plus who were ecstatic to finally hear their boys loud and live. The show had to be stopped for five minutes when too many fans rushed the stage. Gina Wharton of New York was there and recalls the experience, "It was the first concert I ever went to, so it'll always special for that reason. At thirteen, I really had nothing to compare it to, but I remember the screaming was just deafening. My best friend, Monica, and I had said we wouldn't scream. That lasted about thirty seconds after they hit the stage. Eric was so damn dreamy, and I remember wishing I were his guitar so he could hold me close. Monica had been an Alan fan, so I was surprised that she was so into Ian, but she just about fainted when he smiled in her direction. The only song I really remember was 'Money Honey,' 'cause that was my favorite, and I just about died when I heard the first few chords. I saw them again later on the 'It's a Game' tour, but nothing could ever top Atlantic City for me. It was their first show in the country and my first ever, so it was kinda like we lost our virginity together that night—just amazing." Derek Longmuir was happy with the band's performance, declaring victory after the show backstage. "Usually, we're on tour, but this was just a one-nighter, so I think we got by really well."

The next afternoon, June 27, would go down in BCR history as one of the biggest single displays of out-of-control Rollermania. By the *Toronto Star's* next-day estimates, over 65,000 Canadian fans, some of whom spent over twenty-four hours in line, gathered in Toronto's Nathan Phillips Square to see the band at CHUM radio's "Summer Music Festival" event. The original plan was for the group to address the fans from a staging area and for them to be presented with platinum sales awards by their Canadian label, Capitol Records, for *Bay City Rollers* and *Rock 'n' Roll Love Letter*, after brief sets by local opening acts Joe and Bing, Jackson Hawke, and Sweet Blindness. The Rollers wouldn't be playing. But it would be a chance for the boys to "meet and greet" the faithful.

All advance planning went out the window when the crowd grew more and more impatient in the Toronto heat. Scores of teen and pre-teen girls were passing out in the crush of humanity. Event planners had anticipated an attendance of 15,000 or so for the free event. When the numbers had swelled to over four times that amount, all form of crowd control was lost, and for police on the scene, it was frightening. George Davis was on security patrol that day: "I honestly feared the worst. As the throng grew more and more impatient, I worried that someone was going to die. They were just kids, and I really worried about their safety."

Ian Mitchell remembers, "Jimmy decided to give us the day off, as it would give him time to clean up some tracks and to also do basic mixes on what we had done so far. A day off back then was a luxury, and we were all looking forward to a bit of down-time.

Two limos arrived at the Harbor Castle Hotel; one would be the decoy, and we would be in the other. As it turns out, the decoy was not necessary, as all the fans were at the square. Usually there were two to three hundred hanging outside, so security was always tight. We really had no idea what we were going to, except it was a personal appearance. You know, in and out.

"Packed into the limo, we headed to the square. It wasn't a long drive, but we had to go around the long way for one reason or another. It was at that point the security guy in the front seat started getting loud and anxious requests on his radio. He sounded concerned about something. Meanwhile, in the back we were all just talking about what we were going to do with the rest of the free day. I think Les and I were going to go shopping, and Woods and Eric were going to go to the country. I have no idea what Derek had planned.

"The security guard in the front seat was in a panic, and we asked him what was wrong. It was then we found out there were around 65,000 kids at this place and nowhere near the correct amount of police or guards. We hadn't even arrived there yet, and already kids were fainting and trying to mob the stage. We had to drive around for another twenty minutes while more police were brought to the stage area. I think there was an uneasy feeling between us in the back because of the lack of security. No words were exchanged … just an uneasy silence. Finally, we were brought to the back of the stage area and basically told to run like hell up this ramp and into the dressing room. However, no one had told me to turn right at the top of the ramp, and I ran straight on the stage. A large scream quickly turned me in my tracks, and I bolted back and was ushered in the right direction. The band thought I had done it on purpose. But I hadn't. But I had seen the crowd and was very nervous. The rest is kind of a blur as it happened so fast. The chief of police wanted us out of there ASAP.

"We were literally taken from the dressing room to the stage, were we went to the front and started waving and smiling. That's when all hell broke loose. The CHUM radio guy was calling for order. It fell on deaf ears. The barriers at the front buckled, and the next thing I knew we had been hauled off the stage, into the Limo, and back to the hotel in record time. I really think we were all relieved to get out of there." It was then agreed that a conciliatory visit to the radio station to address the fans live on the air was in order, so they headed over to the CHUM studios on Young Street.

When the limo pulled up, it was met with even more hysteria. Roger Ashby, one of the station's disc jockeys, recalls, "The fans had totally covered their limo. When they pulled up to the sidewalk, there was no way they could get out of the car. We were all very worried that the roof would collapse."

It was a fear that was shared by Mike Klenfner, who was one of those trapped inside. "With the Rollers you really did experience something new every day. That was the day I learned what it would feel like to be in a vehicle actually being crushed around you. I'd be lying if I said I wasn't scared."

With the available security being taxed to its limits, Ashby remembers the team effort of the CHUM staff. "We grabbed every available body from the radio station and formed a human chain so that they could get out and have a safe path in to the station. Somehow, they made it in, and it was like just another day in the life for them. They were all very nice and full of energy—happy for our help and support."

The award presentation that was to have taken place at the Square was moved to the Ramada Inn Hotel later that evening, and Ashby recalls it being like no other soiree he ever attended. "Our 'secret' location didn't stay secret for very long. The hotel was packed with young girls. I remember it was the first and only time that I was served milk and peanut butter and jam sandwiches at a cocktail party. Because of all the kids, there wasn't a drop of alcohol to be found." Ashby speaks with obvious pride when discussing his station's involvement with the Rollers. "We played the hell out of their records, and I can say that CHUM was very instrumental in breaking the band in Canada. There were some residual bad vibes over what happened that afternoon. A few people were blaming us for the thing getting out of control, saying, 'Look what you've done here,' but what did you expect, it was what it was, the band were very popular and people wanted to see them and be near them."

After the madness on the 26th, the band adjourned to Soundstage Studios to put the wraps on the *Dedication* album. Jimmy Ienner remembers the track that got the Rollers treatment first after the break: "'Yesterday's Hero' was one that came from my people. We were constantly listening to songs for Blood, Sweat, and Tears or Three Dog Night over the years, so it was the same with the Rollers. John Paul Young had a minor hit with it, and soon after, they offered the song to the Rollers but they passed. Lyrically it just fit. It was a staff member's suggestion this time. We made the decision to record it with a bit of a smile. Not to be serious with it, but to do it with a bit of a wink, staying away from the lament that is written into the lyric. Ninety-nine percent of the girls who were gonna buy the record wouldn't get the irony of it all anyway."

The producer had another vision that came to life in those first few sessions after the near riot in downtown Toronto. Ienner had been rolling tape at the crazed Nathan Phillips Square event, and he put it to use, incorporating some of the audio into the mix of "Yesterday's Hero." The finished version would ultimately feature the Toronto crowd's anticipatory chant of "We Want the Rollers" as its intro, and then again as a rejoin to the chorus with CHUM's Terry Steele imploring the masses to "move back ... back!"

Ienner says, "I had my crew out to record the crowd. It was the emcee, the station DJ, who yelled the 'fuck off' that we purposefully buried in the final mix. It was just him being frustrated with such a crowd ... he was yelling at my guys with their remote gear." As the group wrapped the album and headed back to the U.K., Toronto began to respond to the aftermath of "Hurricane BCR." The newspapers featured scathing letters to the editor debating the merits of Rollermania, and the owners of

Soundstage Studios continued to deal with the never-ending phone calls and studio visits by fans even after the band was gone—a phenomenon that would ultimately force them to make the public statement that the Bay City Rollers and their fans were not welcome back. But they would be back in their adopted Canadian home away from home a few short months later, playing the Maple Leaf Gardens at a sold-out show during their first North American concert tour. For Jimmy Ienner, the experience was one he wouldn't trade for anything. "The residue that I'm left with from the Bay City Rollers is that they were wonderful to work with. I know they wanted me to do their next album too, but there was no way to even begin to fit it in with my schedule at the time. Harry Maslin ended up doing the next one instead. I am saddened by the fact that the seriousness of the issues surrounding them at the time kept them from really getting it done. They were in love with what they were doing, but not with who they had to do it with—the issues with Tam and all. They really wanted this to be their life and deserved to have had things work out better."

With the Rollers' star fading fast in the U.K., and the British press spending more and more time debating the band's sexual preferences and whether or not they were Tam Paton's homosexual playthings, the Rollers stormed through their first brief U.S. tour in mid-August, focusing on the East Coast with shows in Philadelphia, Buffalo, Toronto, Atlanta, and Boston. With them for the whole trip were the husband-and-wife team of Arista's Mike Klenfner and publicist Carol Strauss-Klenfner, who both remember the peculiar ways of Tam Paton. "Tam was a brilliant manager, but there were some things that I can only describe as strange.," Mike Klenfner explained. "He used to tell me that they were all gay. And that he was afraid that this one was going to fall in love with that one. He would book hotel rooms so they would have to share—not just the room, but the bed … king-size beds in all the rooms. Tam said that he'd have to keep switching the roommate situation so they wouldn't fall in love with each other. I can say this without question, my 'gay-dar' wasn't tuned to that in any way at all. They talked about girls constantly. I never saw anything to make me believe any of that."

As the Klenfners continued to serve the band in a professional capacity, they also found themselves at times acting as surrogate parents. Eric and Les even spent a few nights at the Klenfner home, escaping the sameness of the antiseptic hotels for a quick taste of suburban American lifestyle. "It was really all simple and innocent. They wanted two things more than anything: to sleep in separate beds and to eat a chip buttie [a French-fry sandwich], which they were to make famous later on the *Dinah Shore Show*. In fact, to this day I still impress people from Scotland by tellin' em I know how to make one of those. Not that it's all that hard! But, it's a great conversation starter. I remember one night, my wife Carol was sleeping heavy like she always does, so I got up and put my bathrobe on and tiptoed out to see for myself if all the rumors that Tam was feeding me were true. All I saw was a Roller on the couch, a Roller on the floor, both asleep and the kitchen looked like a bomb had gone off with chip buttie mess everywhere. They were just incredibly nice kids, full of enthusiasm and energy. They would work harder than any band I've ever dealt with before or since. They'd do anything you asked. Forget music. To a man, just great human beings, and we had so much fun."

From the comfort of the "Chateau D' Klenfner," it was back to L.A. for more television, including a memorable song and dance routine in white tails and top hats on the Bill Cosby variety show, *Cos*, that took place on Ian Mitchell's eighteenth birthday. That was followed up by the aforementioned appearance on the *Dinah Shore Show* that was forever notable due to Ian's gleeful, over-the-top chip buttie preparation. After pouring almost an entire shaker of salt and half a bottle of catsup on the sandwich, Shore and her co-host, *One Day at a Time* star McKenzie Phillips, came very close to vomiting in live and living color for the national television audience.

Back at '16' magazine headquarters in New York, the Rollers were well on their way to setting the (still-to-be broken) record for consecutive appearances on the magazine's cover. For editor

Danny Fields it was the best of times, as the Bay City Rollers dominated his publication's pages. He told the *New York Daily News*, "Truly, there's no one else. It's not a hype. We're trying to sell magazines to readers from nine to fourteen, and the Rollers are their guys. We get around 15,000 letters a month from Roller fans, and they're by no means saturated here. Our circulation has jumped since we began featuring them." Fields also dismissed the growing allegations that the band and their manager were having their way with each other sexually. But he says that even if they were, he would have never gone public with it. "They knew that I was gay. It's not a secret, and I've been out in the open about that my whole life. Well, at least my whole adult life. It wasn't an issue. I never witnessed anyone in the Bay City Rollers fucking. Rock and roll is sex and drugs, and there is always plenty of that, but what good does it do to expose anything that might or might not be going on? It's not my business to go public with that and why would I have wanted to kill the golden goose? I was never a witness to anything untoward involving the Rollers. In fact, I can say this: Les McKeown, who I was closest to in the band, was relentlessly heterosexual. This band was fun and extremely professional." The relationship with Fields and '16' would eventually anger other teen publishers, most notably the Laufer Publications magazine *Tiger Beat*, who felt that favoritism was being shown to their competitor and began to reduce its coverage of the Rollers. '16's' associate editor, Hedy End, says the writing style of her magazine also had a lot to do with why they were the choice of the true North American Rollermaniac. "At '16,' we took a little different approach than most of the teen magazines. We aimed for a slightly older readership. And it may sound weird, but we almost took a bit of a feminist outlook in our stories. A little more personal and less fluffy. Our stories tried to get a bit more of the personal angle out of the stars we featured—including the Bay City Rollers."

The beginning of September saw the release of the first single from *Dedication*, the Rollers' remake of Dusty Springfield's 1964 smash "I Only Want to Be With You." Bolstered by countless television appearances, the song would eventually find its way in to the top ten on both sides of the Atlantic. But for Britian, it would be their last big hit. Sensing the slipping popularity at home, the group began a run of shows in Dundee on September 9. When the short tour wrapped in New Victoria, London, ten days later, it was pretty much their swan song; from that point forward, the band would focus most of its energy on the U.S., Canada, and Germany, plus the still-unmined territory of Japan and the Far East. It was also at this time that Tam Paton, feeling the heat from the U.K. news media about his sexual preference, announced his "engagement" to London art college student Marcella Knaiflova at a formal dinner, with the band and a dozen select journalists present. Photos of the evening's proceedings and the "happy couple" ran in most of the major publications in the days to follow, and, amazingly, the rumored "Rollers Gay Manager" headlines never appeared. It would be revealed later that Paton's "fiancée" was actually the lesbian lover of the BCR's publicist, Beth Coleman.

In the morale department, the simmering tensions between the group members that had been noticeable in Toronto came to a boil one day at Paton's home in Scotland. Ian Mitchell recalls, "We went back to Edinburgh for a photo session for the *Dedication* cover. We were looking at the shots, and there was a picture that Woody didn't like. His hair was flat on one side or something. Anyway, he threw a total fit over it. I thought it was fine and said so. Woody got all upset and ran out and across the road to this old ruined church building. Eric got right in my face and shouted at me, 'Don't you ever fucking talk to my friend that way!' I went over to where Woody was and apologized to him. He was crying and everything. Then I told Eric I was sorry and that I didn't mean anything by it. They both just figured I was taking Tam's side on the picture thing. It was that tense. Tam would say things like, 'So, you're becoming buddies now,' and I'd think well … yeah. We *are* in a band together here." It was becoming apparent to Mitchell that his time in the band would be short lived. "By the time *Dedication* came out, the group was on the way down in the U.K., and Tam just couldn't or wouldn't see it. It got to be a real drag. I was thinking of leaving right then. Les was too. He said we should quit together, but that we should wait and give it a month or two."

With the *Dedication* album selling briskly around the world, and with more American television planned for mid-October, Woody and Ian were hospitalized together at the beginning of the month for much needed procedures. For Wood it was minor sinus surgery to correct a problem that was affecting his hearing. Mitchell went under the knife to remove two small nodes from his vocal cords. Once recuperated, it was back to Los Angeles to tape another *Midnight Special*, the *Tony Orlando and Dawn Show*, and another installment of *Merv Griffin*. With November earmarked for a major tour to include New Zealand, Australia, and Japan, the group took a planned holiday at the end of the month. Ian and Derek ended up in Barbados together, Woody spent his time off in Montego Bay, Jamaica, Les took his parents to Luxembourg—where they visited DJ friend Peter Powell—and Eric stayed home in London.

It was in the days that followed that short vacation that Mitchell made up his mind; he was fed up with being a Bay City Roller and wanted out. He says, "We had started writing for *It's a Game*. Derek was staying at Tam's house. Les called and wanted me to come pick him up in my Mini. We ended up at his brother Ronnie's club—a place called Maestro's. I pulled a chick and we went back to her house for a shag at like four in the morning. A few hours later, it's still dark out. I'm driving my car and I ask this bobby if he could tell me where the Edinburgh Road is. He says give me a ride and I'll give you directions. I drop him off at the police station and he says, 'You're Ian Mitchell, right?' I say 'yeah,' and he thanks me for the ride. I had so much alcohol still in my system he could have totally busted me for public intoxication, but he didn't. Imagine those headlines. Well, just as I get back, Derek's leaving for the studio. He asked me where I'd been and whether I was coming in. I told him I'd probably go later. And that was it. I went in to Tam's house and packed my shit. I called Tam in London and said, 'I'm leaving.' I'll never forget what he said: "Grab Damian (former bandmate Damian McKee), go to Barbados, and don't say anything to the press.' He just didn't get it it at all. From that moment on, I was an ex-Bay City Roller."

The decision came as a shock to the band, who'd figured that he would at least stick around long enough to get through the upcoming Far East tour. But in the press, Paton was unusually pragmatic, saying to *Parade Magazine*, "If Ian had stuck it out with the Rollers for another year, even if he wasn't too happy he could have been a millionaire. But, I guess it's better to be happy than a dead pop star."

The outgoing Mitchell, showing maturity that belied his birth certificate, explained, "What does money matter when your sanity is at stake? The pressures I've undergone these last six months, you can't believe it. At times, I almost felt like committing suicide. A Rollers life is enough to drive one mad. I found myself walking the streets at three in the morning from our hotel because I couldn't wind down. I'm happy to be away from it all. When you're a pop star, the pressures are immense. Some can put up with it. Frankly, I can't. When we weren't on stage, we were locked up together inside four walls. I got more and more depressed as each day went on."

Mitchell was swiftly replaced. Patrick James McGlynn (b. 3/31/58) had already been handpicked by Tam Paton. With Ian Mitchell's abrupt departure, the eighteen-year-old Edinburgh guitarist was introduced to the press as a Roller ahead of schedule. McGlynn says, "I had been in a band called 'Wot's Up' with Woody. Then my brother and I started the Pat McGlynn Band. It was just after that I came to meet Tam Paton. He kept in touch—kind of like a prison officer, calling and checking on me all the time. The plan was for me to join the Rollers after Japan and become the sixth member. Then, Ian quit and I was in. I remember passing him in the hallway at Tam's, and he wished me luck and said I'd be lucky to make it six months. Two weeks after becoming a Roller, I was off on a world tour." Meanwhile, Ian Mitchell returned to his old group, now known as Rosetta Stone, in Ireland, happy with his decision but regretting the fact that his band's manager would still be Tam Paton. "We were contractually obligated to Tam or there is no way in hell I would have had him manage Rosetta Stone. We just had no other fucking choice."

Tam Paton used the McGlynn introduction as an opportunity to answer the critics who were blasting him over the constant turnover and image of purity that had been belied by his own admitted use of tranquilizers and Faulkner's accidental overdose, saying, "It's all rubbish. Three of them smoke, they drink what they want, and Eric has a flat in London where he can take whom he likes. He might have four wives there for all I know." Continuing to defend his actions, the angry manager said, "They have no respect musically from you people and this depresses them. They have become prisoners who can't even go for a walk without being mobbed. Maybe there have been times when I've driven them a bit hard. I suppose, one day, they'll say I was a lousy manager." Sid Bernstein, sensing the press were turning on the group that he'd promised to sell out Shea Stadium with, chose the same time frame to sue Paton for abrogation of contract and past royalties due. As the lawyers for both sides tackled that issue, the group and their new guitar player packed their suitcase for a liaison with the Far East.

In late November the Bay City Rollers headed off to the tour that would solidify a love affair with the Japanese that continues to this day. After successful shows in New Zealand and Australia, they were met in Japan with a reaction that equaled—and at times exceeded—that of Britain in '75, or even Toronto earlier in the year. It was the same at every show: Tokyo, Kyoto, Kyushu, Osaka … critics be damned, Rollermania was back and louder than ever in Japan. Hundreds of reporters turned out at the press conferences, and, through an interpreter, the band made it clear again and again that they loved the reaction of the Japanese fans. Derek Longmuir said, "It's just incredible here. We knew that they liked our music, but we weren't sure what to expect at the shows. It's been really fun and completely crazy in Japan." The trip was not to be without controversy. Les McKeown claims that it was while they were in Japan that he found out from Pat McGlynn how the others felt about him. He then purchased surveillance devices and placed the bugs in their rooms. "They weren't very nice about it at all, there were lots of expletives. I don't understand why, to tell you the truth. I know I'm cheeky and I get up people's nose, but I don't understand why someone who has made their life better should be held in such, you know, euuch."

Despite the James Bond-like discovery, the group's overall spirits were buoyed by the fan reaction. The land of the rising sun was now officially the land of the rising Rollers. It was time for a quick Christmas break at home and for Arista to release "Yesterday's Hero" as the second single from *Dedication*. The first week of the New Year would find the group back in L.A. for their West Coast concert debut at the Santa Monica Civic Auditorium, and in New York to play their first show there at the Palladium. It was now 1977, or as Pat McGlynn would later refer to it, "my time in hell."

NINE

And Then There Were Four

Pat McGlynn shared a lot of common ground with the man he replaced in the Rollers. They were both from solid families, around the same age, and both had been on Tam Paton's "radar screen" prior to their joining the band. Beyond those similarities, they were both thrust into the Bay City Roller maelstrom with little advance rehearsal for their big moment. Unlike Mitchell, who seemed to fit right in despite the pressure, McGlynn behaved like an outsider from the start. Stand-offish in person and looking disinterested in performance, he seemed to be in a constant daze—never really quite there. All this despite the fact that most who really knew him said that as a musician, he was already on a par or ahead of his bandmates in terms of raw ability. A member of Glasgow's Average White Band was quoted as saying, "Pat McGlynn had chops, even then. If he hadn't joined the Rollers he could have easily played guitar in just about any Scottish band in the '70s. He was funky, and I'm not sure that even he knew how good he was."

According to McGlynn, his initial disappointment came from the instant realization that his desire to assert himself musically would be thwarted from the outset. "The music meant nothing to Tam; it was all about publicity. Interviews, TV shows, and photo sessions. Not at all what I thought I was signing up for in that regard." To complicate things, McGlynn would later contend that he was getting the wrong kind of attention from Paton. More on that subject in a bit.

January was a busy time for the Bay City Rollers. "Yesterday's Hero" had stiffed, failing to crack the top forty on either side of the Atlantic. *Dedication* was released as the next single, with Les re-recording Ian's vocals from the album version. The back-to-back shows on January 7 and 8 in Santa Monica and New York were well received. Both shows were complete sell-outs and got favorable reviews. It was at the Palladium in New York where former road manager Jake Duncan met up with the band backstage and was offered his old job back. He accepted on the spot. "I was working in upstate New York," says Duncan. "I came down to check out the guys at the Palladium and met up with them after. It was evident that things had changed. Eric was deep in a power struggle with Les and the label. He just resented any shift that would go his way. Pat McGlynn was in now and didn't seem to fit in. Really, just off his face. But, on the bright side, they were a smaller operation than say, Aerosmith, whom I had been working with, and it was an opportunity to call some shots, so, with the guys assuring me that good things were coming, especially in the States, where they were planning on doing four to five-thousand seaters, I accepted the position of tour manager."

The band stayed in Manhattan at the Warwick and Essex hotels for next three days, meeting with Clive Davis and producer Harry Maslin (David Bowie), who had been selected to replace Jimmy Ienner for their next album. Using the recent failure of the last two singles to do anything, the group convinced Davis and Maslin that they should use more of their own material. Eric offered up demos for another six songs, and McGlynn shared that he had also been writing. After appearing on Bob McAllister's *Wonderama* children's show, it was another *Mike Douglas* taping in Philadelphia, then after a few weeks in London, they returned for an entire week with Douglas as his special co-hosts from Miami.

It was in Miami that McGlynn says the bubble began to burst. Reiterating charges that he made public in the British press in early 2003, McGlynn says, "I started having regrets right away. Tam was after my ass from the start. The first night I was in the band, he tried to give me a wank on the couch, and it just got worse with him from there. Once or twice a week he'd try something. The band wasn't any better. They treated me like shit, figuring I was just the next wee boy they could abuse. It was non-stop harassment. After a couple of weeks I figured out that Les was the only guy in the band that was normal, and it became he and I, two rebels against the world and Tam."

McGlynn claims that by the time the group finished in Japan and went to the States, he'd begun to use drugs to deal with the pressure that was being applied to him. "With what Tam was pulling on me, drugs were the only way to cope. When I joined, I was just a kid from a working-class family. We were literally gypsies, and I was experienced in a street sense but had never done a drug in my life. I mean, we raised horses and I worked my Dad's land until I joined the Rollers. It started with amphetamines and led to cocaine. Tam said I was fattish and needed to lose weight. Have you seen my pictures? I was very thin. Losing weight is not why he wanted me to be high. I remember being in Miami for the *Mike Douglas Show*, and he was plying me with the stuff. Just piles of coke. It got so bad I was actually sleeping with my clothes on just in case he would try something in the middle of the night. Finally, on our trip home we stayed in New York and he tried twice. The second time, I was ready for him. I kept a bread knife under my pillow, and when he came for me, I stabbed him with it in the shoulder, and that was the last time he tried."

It should be noted that McGlynn's claims of abuse at the hands of his manager and bandmates were denied vehemently by Tam Paton, who, when presented with the accusations made by the guitarist, responded by saying, "Mr. McGlynn was looked after well during his time in the Rollers, but now he's living in fantasy land. This is ridiculous. I can tell you there is absolutely no truth in the allegations that he is making whatsoever." He then added, "It's a load of crap. Certainly never had any sexual relations with him. I'm afraid he wasn't my scene. I like men, but I'm not into boys. I don't have any stab wounds or anything. Before the band was ever famous, we traveled around the country and we did share rooms. You had to rent twin-bedded rooms, but I never shared rooms with the band when Pat McGlynn was there. I never shared a room with McGlynn. It's a new one on me." The only Roller to comment on McGlynn's version of events after it hit the papers was Les McKeown, who denied any first-hand knowledge but does say in his 2003 autobiography *Shang A Lang* that he remembers McGlynn running in to his room to get away from Paton.

'*16*' magazine's Danny Fields was in Miami for the whole week and doesn't recall anything happening between the two. "I never saw any of that. Pat was just kind of non-existent to me. Les was cool. I've always like lead singers. I remember him and me, literally sitting on the dock of the bay in Miami, smoking pot and listening to Pink Floyd. It wasn't Danny from '*16*' magazine and Leslie of the Bay City Rollers. It was just two guys talking about life. Getting philosophical. I found him to be the most interesting of them all. Probably because he was the opposite of me. He was very outgoing and bright. Eric Faulkner was very charming. He'd go out of his way to be diplomatic. Very serious about the music. Derek was quiet. Woody was delightful and sweet. What you saw is what you got with Woody. Thoroughly British, and winsome. He had a natural charm. Like I said, Pat and Ian were just interchangeable to me ... the interchangeable twinkies. I make it a point to really never get close to more than two members of a traveling rock and roll crew. Any more than that is dangerous. You start getting into this one wanting to know what that one said about this one. Les and Tam, their manager, was pretty much who I connected with, and I don't remember any thing nasty happening."

With Toronto no longer an option, the Rollers chose Gothenburg Sweden's Tal and Ton Studios as home base for the recording of their next album, *It's a Game,* in February 1977. Working with Maslin, assistant engineer Martin Pearson, and arranger Barry "Foz" Fasman (Melissa Manchester, Diana Ross, Billy Joel), the group resolved to move their sound into a more adult direction. Strings and horns were more evident than before, and once again the choice of material ended being a fifty/fifty split between covers and originals. Whether that was the band's choice or Clive Davis and Arista Records exercising their creative control clause is debatable. Davis addressed the issue, saying, "Some of their biggest hits were written by people outside of the group. I find that what is key is the material. What happens is that artists forget who wrote the material and then, they decide that they want to be the next Bob Dylan. They just assumed then that they could pick up the mantle and write, and that was never their forte."

Nonetheless, the Rollers tackled "When I Say I Love You (The Pie)"—a band favorite from fellow Scots the Sutherland Brothers—Len Boone's "You Made Me Believe in Magic," "Harvey Shield's "The Way I Feel Tonight," "Love Power" by Teddy Vann (A hit for the Sandpebbles in 1967 and later a huge smash for Luther Vandross), "It's a Game" (String Driven Thing, 1973) by Chris Adams, and, with a nod to producer Maslin, an Eric Faulkner-sung cover of David Bowie's *Diamond Dogs* rocker "Rebel Rebel." Band originals included the Pat McGlynn co-written "Sweet Virginia," the Faulkner/Wood-penned "Love Fever," "Dance, Dance, Dance," and "Don't Let the Music Die." Finally, Les McKeown helped Eric and Woody finish "Inside a Broken Dream."

For Harry Maslin, the task ahead was to maintain the rock sensibility of the band and, at the same time, to assist them in growing their sound with the audience. "They were definitely open to new ideas and great to work with. All of the frustrations they were feeling were put aside so we could make a great record. I appreciated their desire to try new things vocally and otherwise, and their eagerness. Woody even tried to learn the sax—in fact, I think he may still have one of mine."

Engineer Fasman says he had very little interaction with the group. "It was all very cursory. They were a lot of fun, and I thought just a great bunch of guys. Most of what I brought to the table came afterwards, in L.A. I think Harry just felt comfortable with me after the success we had together with 'Don't Cry Out Loud' by Melissa, and the Eric Carmen album; they just wanted some of that maturity to be added to the mix with the Rollers. I'm still very proud of 'The Way I Feel Tonight'; I think it was one of their best."

The months of March and April found the band putting the final touches to the album in Switzerland and taking advantage of their close proximity to Germany to maximize face-time there, collecting awards from *Melodie der Veldt*, Radio Luxembourg, and *Bravo*, and taping the *Disco '77* and *Pop '77* television shows. Mixing sessions continued throughout April, and then Pat McGlynn received a phone call at home from his bandmates letting him know that his services would no longer be required. After only five short months, he was no longer a Bay City Roller—a decision that McGlynn says actually came as a relief. "We had a promotion meeting to discuss the plan for the album release and the tour. I was at my place getting ready to leave for *Top of the Pops*, and I got a call from Eric and Woody. They called to tell me I was out. They sacked me over the phone. They actually sang 'Bye Bye Baby' down the damn phone to me to rub it all in. I laughed at them and told them I was delighted to be out."

With *It's a Game* practically finished and the title track chosen as the first European single, Maslin and his crew went into damage control mode immediately after being notified of McGlynn's departure. The decision was made to wipe and re-record all of the guitarist's playing and vocals and to excise his photo from the nearly completed artwork. McGlynn remains bitter about that to this day. "I did my job and got nothing for it. I was playing great and writing, but it wasn't about that. Bay City Music was the publishing company, and that was a total rip-off. I wrote three songs on the *It's a Game* album—'Dance, Dance, Dance,' 'Love Fever,' and 'Sweet Virginia'—and got no credit at all. Derek Longmuir got songwriting credit and he wasn't even there." The official word from "Camp BCR" was that Pat McGlynn wasn't fitting in. His statements to the press at the time said the reasons were financial; McGlynn claimed that as a member of an internationally famous rock band, he should have been paid more than £20 per week. Getting the real truth depends on whom you speak to. While McGlynn has since changed his story and pins it all on a predatory Paton, others continue to speculate. In the years since his abrupt departure, his leaving has been attributed to, among other things, excessive drug use and a sexual escapade with Maslin's wife. No matter, in 1977, the task of "de-McGlynning" the *It's a Game* album would be considerable, and, without a finished product, the suddenly four-piece rock group arrived in New York to begin rehearsals for their first full-scale American tour without an album to tour behind. The show, it was decided, must and would go on.

New York's Westchester Theater was the first stop on the trek on May 9. From there, it was on to Boston, Poughkeepsie, Philadelphia, Pittsburgh, Wheeling, Erie, Toledo, Cleveland, Dayton, and Chicago, where the band judged a dance contest between games of a White Sox doubleheader at Comiskey Park. That was followed by stops in Waterloo, Minneapolis, Omaha, Dallas, Oklahoma City, Denver, Salt Lake City, Berkeley, San Jose, Anaheim, and finally San Diego on June 4th. A second leg of outdoor shows was announced for late summer with concerts planned for fairs and festivals in the South and Midwest. Pat McGlynn, now an ex-Roller, quickly parlayed his time in the Bay City Rollers into a solo record deal. His first single, a remake of the Turtles' "She'd Rather Be With Me" was recorded and released on Decca in Europe and Japan before the summer was over.

That single and Alan Longmuir's first solo effort, "I'm Confessing," were both unable to crack the charts anywhere. After hosting NBC's *Midnight Special* and having an entire *American Bandstand* show devoted to them, the Rollers reconvened the It's a Game tour a few days after the death of Elvis Presley in August. The tour plowed on through the hot summer months with shows in Montana, Columbus, Youngstown, Detroit, Charlotte, and Louisville, among others. On August 26, the band was presented with keys to the city on "Bay City Roller

Day" in Bay City, Michigan. A larger-than-life wall mural was unveiled downtown, insuring their presence would remain in their namesake city long after they departed for the U.K. at the end of the tour. On December 17, the Rollers shared the stage at the Boston Garden with fellow teen idols Andy Gibb and Shaun Cassidy for a charity concert. Those in attendance say it was the single loudest crowd the city had ever seen or heard. The year ended with the band's *Greatest Hits* package on plenty of Christmas lists, and the decision was made to begin recording their next album in early 1978 at the famous "Mountain Studios" in Montreaux, Switzerland. Alan Longmuir would be "un-retir-ing" after two years to rejoin the band for the project. "The guys said why don't you come back and lend some support," says Longmuir. "I didn't want to let them down." The fab five would also be reunited with producer Harry Maslin. As 1978 began, all was once again rosy in Roller land … well, for a minute anyway.

TEN

Egotrippin' on LSD
(Lead Singer Disease)

As the Rollers wrapped sessions for the *Strangers in the Wind* album, the atmosphere in the studio was nothing less than icy. Faulkner and Wood were having more and more issues with Les, and even though Alan Longmuir was back in the fold, tension was everywhere. Says Wood, "We weren't having any fun at all. It was so negative. I imagine it was a lot like any band that's come to the end of their rope, the Beatles or whoever. It didn't feel like we were even really a band at that time. And, if you listen to it, it's obvious. It was a terrible record. So depressing." McKeown informed the group that he was done and that this would be their last album, and it may have all ended there if it hadn't been for a phone call and subsequent visit from American children's television producer Marty Krofft.

Krofft and his brother Sid were the guiding forces behind successful Saturday morning fare like *Lidsville* and *H.R. Puffenstuff*. After being rebuffed by Swedish pop group Abba, at the last minute, they approached Tam Paton and the Bay City Rollers with the idea of being the centerpiece of their newest NBC project, *The Krofft Superstar Hour*. The band would lip-sync in simulated concert sequences and then interact with the Krofft characters, including Puffenstuff, Witchie Poo, and Mister

123

Munchie. At first the group bristled at the idea, but the desperation brought on by the Abba rejection sweetened the already large pot into an offer that they couldn't refuse. It was a firm thirteen-week commitment, and the tapings would begin in July at KTLA studios in Los Angeles. The breakup would have to wait. There was money to be made—and lots of it. But it wouldn't be an easy undertaking. The Rollers' Scots accents made them almost impossible to understand for the American audience, and they had no real acting abilities. No matter; dialogue and acting coaches were hired, and taping began on schedule with Les McKeown's "diva dial" turned up to eleven. He was the star as far as he was concerned, and he made sure to let everyone involved know it. Tam Paton recalls, "Les was on a total power trip. Out of his head on coke, fucking Rod Stewart's ex-girlfriend, Britt Eckland, and had lots of people telling him what he should or shouldn't do. There was definitely a problem with he and Eric. The others weren't much help in keeping the peace; they all sided with Eric 'cause he was the noisy one. Les had separate cars, rooms, security, and just wanted nothing to do with them beyond work."

While Paton and the band moved into a private residence on Laurel Canyon Road owned by Marty Krofft, McKeown insisted on his own digs at Hollywood's Chateau Marmont. The internal divisions were maintained on the set as Les demanded his own dressing room away from the others and required the constant companionship of road manager Jake Duncan. "I was his personal babysitter," recalls Duncan. "He wanted to be anywhere but with the band. We spent many an hour drowning in his sorrows at Carlos and Charlie's when we should have been at KTLA doing the show."

With the meter running and production costs rising, he would often show up late or not at all and, occasionally, vanish altogether. Says Marty Krofft, "He'd disappear now and then. We've got like a hundred people on the stage. The other guys were trying their best. I think he caused a lot of problems for them."

Bob Levinson, the Rollers publicist at the time, agreed that McKeown had become a handful saying; "The only real problem we had, and it was a big one, was Les and his ego. Strutting like a rock star, which is common with lead singers who confuse the band's success with their own, and that was definitely the major issue."

Derek Longmuir concurred. "We were committed to the show, and we just wanted to be professional, and then he would walk in, two hours late."

Predictably, the end result was beyond bad. Critics pounced on the project. The *Los Angeles Times* called it "the lowest of lows ever achieved in the name of entertainment." And that was one of the kinder quotes. Today, the band members are all in agreement. Les Mckeown said, "The American TV show contributed greatly to the group breaking up. I was completely pissed off. It just reeked of ... crap."

Says Wood, "It was a good experience, I guess. But, it was a Vegas thing. We weren't going down the right road. It was wrong and taking us further and further away. I don't think we made a very careful decision, but we weren't really asked either. Well, we were, but it was very much Tam saying, 'This will be great for you.' Tam was still in the driver's seat at that point. Personally, it's hard to say anything bad about Tam 'cause he made the band successful with the way he marketed us, but looking back on the TV show, it wasn't so wise."

Derek Longmuir understands McKeown's mindset now, telling VH1, "Les never wanted to do the show in the first place. In hindsight, he was probably right."

Marty Krofft is still stinging from the experience. "The biggest mistake I ever made was getting on that plane to Scotland to sign those kids. Their lead singer was impossible. I still question to this day whether they sang any of their songs themselves. That was probably one of my worst experiences, to deal with that group. Nothing but trouble."

Arista released "Where Will I Be Now," a mid-tempo "You Made Me Believe in Magic" clone, in North America and the Faulkner/Wood ballad "All of the World Is Falling in Love" in the

U.K. as the first singles from *Strangers in the Wind*. All were met with a collective yawn. The LP, a fifty/fifty split between group compositions and outside material, was even more orchestrated than *It's a Game* had been. Buried in strings and lacking anything resembling the rock and roll sensibilities of their previous releases, the album was a commercial and critical disaster. *People Weekly* called it "… absolute MOR dreck. The worst album of the year … bar none." The final single, "Another Rainy Day in New York City" never saw the light of day commercially. It was released to radio only, and never got played.

On the final day of taping, McKeown was blasted in the face by a "pie assassin" with a whipped cream pie, courtesy of his perturbed bandmates. It was a metaphor for the frustrations felt by cast and crew alike. And it was a fitting end to what had been a completely frustrating period for all. With the television commitment out of the way, the band members went their separate ways for what most figured would be the last time. No one wanted to continue. If it wasn't the end of the line, you could see it from there.

ELEVEN

Wham! Glam! Fuck You, Tam!

Back in London, Tam Paton continued in his attempt to salvage the Bay City Rollers as a viable entity. The group's coffers were low, and with the failure of the album and television series, he was looking for a quick cash infusion. He got it in, of all places, Japan. Similarly to the Krofft proposition, a famous Japanese promoter, Mr. Udo, had offered a substantial sum for a Rollers tour. With their career virtually dead everywhere else, the band agreed to go and grab the bucks while they were on the table. The "Les vs. the rest" issues continued to be a problem. And it all came to an ugly head on stage in Osaka.

"Before the show," recalls Paton, "Les had sent a note to the other dressing room for his 'backing group.' He had spelled out the program for the night. He wanted them to open without him, do three or four numbers, and then he would come on, do three or four, and leave. The others were having none of it, and eventually I talked Les out of that idea. I left for a while and came back when they were due to be finishing and was met by a police officer who said I must stop the show. It had become very violent, which I hadn't realized. Then the Mr. Udo was screaming at me. I wasn't sure why. But I soon found out."

Jake Duncan also witnessed the Osaka implosion. "They had been contracted for big money to do these shows in Japan. Eric and Les were at the peak of their problems. Eric's one vocal turn was during 'Rebel Rebel.' We would stack the ground fill in such a way that he could take two steps and be on top of them. He'd be givin' it big licks on top of the speaker stack with the spotlight on him. Leslie decided to get on top of the stack on the other side of the stage, figuring 'I'll take some of that spotlight,' and then all hell broke loose. Les and Woody started shoving and pushing each other. Eric grabs Les to go offstage and have words, leaving the other three to fill. No lead vocals or guitar for like twenty minutes. Then it was lights on and pandemonium. They all left angry, and later I saw our road crew chief, John Gorman, in the bar at Les's hotel. He said that McKeown had ordered 'drinks for the house' and that he had been forced to sign for them after Les left to the tune of four thousand pounds. Lots of happy, drunken Japanese businessmen. Of course, that was charged to the band's account, and it was over the next day as far as Les being in the group."

Paton says it was at that point that he too wanted out. "I didn't choose sides, but it was sad to see them dying. Rosetta Stone needed my attention. I went from Japan to my office in London. I get a letter from Les saying that he was out and that I wasn't his manager anymore. Things had changed so much."

McKeown's version varies from Paton's. To his mind, he was fired and left holding the bag. "I got a bill from American Express for £24,000. And I thought that's weird, 'cause it usually never comes to my house, it usually goes to the bank and always just gets cleared. It wasn't until that time that I found out that because of the power of attorney I'd given Tam Paton that he was able to open and close [my] bank accounts because he could act on my behalf." So, after five years as the front man of the Bay City Rollers, Les McKeown was out. He quickly returned to London to begin work on his first solo album, *All Washed Up*, with his new best friend and confidant, British songwriter Scobie Ryder. Their collaboration would eventually use the ironic moniker of "Les McKeown's Ego Trip." The others, buoyed by their mutual disgust for the departed singer, vowed to continue and began the search for his immediate replacement.

Twenty-one-year-old (b.12/16/56) Duncan Caldwell Faure (pronounced "Four-Uh") grew up in Pretoria, South Africa. The product of a solid middle class upbringing, his parents encouraged his creativity from the start, shuttling him to gigs with his first band, "Orange Cashboat," when he was too young to drive. Talent ran in the family; his older brother, Bill, was one of the country's most successful television and film directors (*Dingley's Bookshop, Shaka Zulu*). By the age of nineteen, Duncan was a member of South African rock group Rabbitt, a four-piece outfit that included future Yes guitarist Trevor Rabin. They had been the biggest English-speaking act that the country had ever produced. After getting reaction throughout their homeland similar to the hysteria associated with the Bay City Rollers, the band broke up in 1977 when an American launch failed and Rabin left to go solo. Faure was being managed by DeMann and groomed for his own solo career when the Bay City Rollers opportunity presented itself.

Faure says, "It was November, 1978. My package had found its way into Eric's hands. He called my agent Bill Trout's office and set up a meeting with Freddy and I and Clive Davis at the Beverly Hills Hotel. I played three songs on acoustic guitar. The next day I had a first-class ticket to Dublin. It was at the Grisham Hotel in Dublin where I first met the Rollers and, eventually, Tam Paton. We got on like long-lost brothers immediately." Eric Faulkner was especially keen on adding a member who, unlike McKeown, could not only sing but was also a songwriter and multi-instrumentalist. He could play guitar and keyboards and had an eerily Lennon-esque vocal quality that Beatles-fan Faulkner fell for in a big way. This guy was different, and after all the drama, that was a good thing.

The Rollers wasted no time making Faure feel welcome. "They gave me everything. They bought me a $7,000 electric piano. They bought me a radio microphone, a two-hundred-watt double stack [of] Marshalls ... everything. You name it ... clothes, I couldn't believe it; 'here's a thousand pounds, go buy some leather jackets.'"

Tam Paton wasn't so sure about the change. "They introduce me to this guy 'from L.A.' and I said hi. He said hi, and then I said, 'You don't have an American accent.' He says, 'No, I'm from South Africa.' My first reaction was to blurt out 'Oh fuck!' I had booked the band for a German tour—thirteen dates—and there was no way they were gonna let a guy with a South African passport into Germany. This was at the peak of apartheid. I tried to talk the band into getting Les back for the tour and told them that if they wanted Duncan for recording or whatever after that I'd get his issues sorted out. They were having none of it. 'No way, Tam! We are the band and you are our servant, get him a visa now!'

"I tried with every connection I had ... international lawyers, everything. They all said it would take at least a year even for an Irish passport. But the band was so headstrong about it, they went anyway. Sure enough, three shows in, I get a call from Barry Evangalist—who was handling the tour—and he says 'I have to get out of here. They want Duncan to leave, and they're telling promoters to fuck off.' I told him to get on a plane the next morning and tell Jake you're leaving. That night, Alan and Woods call and tell me to 'get my fat ass over to Germany and fix these problems or you're sacked.' I told them that I couldn't and wouldn't be coming over. I hung up the phone and turned to [live-in partner] Raymond [Cotter] and said, 'We'll sleep good tonight, it's over.' The next day, Derek calls and begs me not to quit, but I'd had it. Glad to put that chapter of my life behind me."

TWELVE

Ride My Fibrillator

With Rollermania, sold-out concerts, and the covers of teen magazines a distant memory, the group spent the latter part of 1978 and early 1979 globe-hopping to introduce their new lineup and look. Other than an occasional scarf, the tartan had virtually disappeared, as had the words "Bay City" from their name. Now simply known as "the Rollers," the group visited Germany, where the new lineup found itself literally bumping into their former lead singer at an awards ceremony. It didn't take long for it to get ugly. Eric Faulkner recalled, "We finished our set and Les jumped on stage and tried to steal the show. It totally backfired, because no one was interested. I didn't see the sense in it." Later in the hotel lobby, they crossed paths again. Alan Longmuir, still seething from the incident at the awards show, was having none of it. "Les just rushed forward to Woody and walloped him between the shoulder blades. I got so mad, I ran over and grabbed him by the scruff of the neck and punched him three times in the face. It was only when he was lying on the ground that I came to my senses. It's just as well; he's wee-er than me, or I would have hit him some more."

Woody Wood made his distaste for McKeown public, saying, "Les McKeown is the only person I know with hemorrhoids coming out of his mouth."

From Germany it was on to the U.S. (three times) and the U.K.. Most of January was spent writing and rehearsing in London, and from there, they hunkered down in Ireland's Dublin Sound Studios. The sounds that were being created were unlike anything the group had produced since *Rock 'n' Roll Love Letter.* The album, to be called *Elevator,* was produced by Peter Ker (the Motors) and found the band rocking hard. New front man Duncan Faure contributed four songs, Faulkner two, and the band collaborated on the other six. Faulkner and Faure carried the bulk of the co-writing duties, an arrangement that worked well according to Faure. "We're the two that write more than the others. A lot of the time, we write together. We'll get together and say 'hey, I've got this,' and we'll put it together, or we'll be sitting, jamming a bit and suddenly he'll go home and do something or I'll go home and do something and we'll put it together later. *Elevator* was like that. I wrote the verse and intro, and Eric did the chorus."

What all of the new material had in common was a renewed spirit and energy that had been sorely missed. Faure says the atmosphere was conducive to good work. "The guys are so relaxed and happy-go-lucky. Woody thinks positive all the time, and I've learned a lot from him because when you think positive, things around you happen positively, and as soon as you think negative, things around you happen negatively. Everybody's happy and positive, and it's great." The team concept was not lost on Faure, who says he was treated like an equal from jump street. "They could have said, when I joined the band, 'Hey listen, it's our name, it's our band, here's nineteen for me and one for you,' but it wasn't the case at all. They said, 'You're out there on the road working as hard as we are and so it's the same money.' Right from the first day I came in, when the guys got a one-dollar bill, I got one dollar." With everyone pulling together as a unit, the Rollers remained focused on the task at hand. There was a firm commitment on the part of the band to reestablish itself musically. Faure recalls, "The sessions were brilliant. Peter was perfect for us. He had a bit of a new wave punk energy that we all fed off of. Voices were all in shape, and the band was tight."

The critics agreed. *Trouser Press* called the album "a delightful surprise; great power pop, so much more straight ahead than any other Rollers record." *Billboard* and *Sounds* both praised the LP's first single, the Faulkner/Faure/Wood/Alan Longmuir-penned "Turn on the Radio," with the latter choosing it as their single of the week." There was no doubt about it: the group had a new lease on life.

"It feels like playing in a new band," said Wood. "We've been through all the hassles and we're all positive now. It's the first time we've had a good time making an album, first time in a long, long time."

A newly shorn and mustachioed Faulkner added, "The music has always taken a back seat to the image; we're finally happy doing things we want to happen." He also pointed out that the change in front men was welcome and maybe overdue. "The group has to come first. That was one of the things we could never get through to Les. With him it was always looking after number one. I was glad to be rid of him in the end, because it just wasn't working. I've got arguments with the guy, but I wish him all the best. I see no reason for backsniping—it's pointless. We've got our story, he's got his."

With McKeown in the rearview mirror and the the group in total creative control for the first time, Faulkner admitted that the success or failure of the project sat squarely on their shoulders, saying, "At least if it bombs now, it's our fault. That will be much easier to stomach."

Derek Longmuir said the changes were a result of the band's determination to work hard as a unit. "We were always hard workers, and we survived [the changes] because we were a group. We did more of our own writing this time and worked hard on our sound, determined to grow up along with the audience we had built for ourselves."

Faure acknowledged the change in direction, adding, "We've found with the new sound that the music has really grown up. There's none of the teenybopper thing anymore. The Rollers have grown up a lot. It's no longer just a young group. I mean, we're now rock and rollers. We're not a punk rock band, I must admit, I really got into that in a way because you'd get all these young guys who were just starting bands and making early rock and roll again. We're sort of melodic new wave. The girls are no longer fifteen, they're like nineteen or twenty and bringing along their boyfriends of twenty and twenty-one. The thing is, you'll never get a [Rolling] Stones audience that would appreciate the Rollers and, it'll be the same thing once the Rollers are thirty-five years old, you'll never get a Rollers audience going for a new kid band. I feel that we've put our heads together and come up with a very 'today'-sounding album. For me, personally, I think it's the best album I've ever been involved with, so I'm really proud of it." Hopes were high that the group's fan base would accept the changes with open arms.

Whether that was possible remained to be seen. With the original BCR fans now in their late teens and into bands like the Cars, the Clash, and Blondie, the true test would be whether or not they would accept the new look and sound of the Rollers. Based on the tepid sales of the album and the lack of promotion and airplay for "Radio," the answer was a resounding "no." Frustrating. Especially when coupled with the group's inability to attract any new pre-teen fans. Bob Levinson explains how daunting that task was from a publicist's point of view; "the teen mags were already on to someone else. Remember, the base audience was thirteen to fifteen years old. Those first kids had moved on to whatever. And for the new teens, it was KISS. Which took everybody by surprise. The formula was always cute kids who were a bit feminine and non-threatening. KISS changed all of that, the whole choreography of the teen idol dance. As far as the new crop of teens were concerned, The Bay City Rollers were their older sister's band. Problem was, older sister wasn't into them anymore. The band tried, but they had so much working against them. Playlists were tightening and in those days, without radio, you had nothing. Who would play it? It was a heck-of-a predicament. The line you were always hearing from the guys was 'we want the audience to grow with us.' The nature of the beast is that things change, tastes change, and it's constant."

Faure puts some of the blame on the band for trying to grow too fast, too soon. "It backfired, we were uncool to the older kids and too cool for the younger ones. Woody and Eric had that 'Stoned Houses' bit at the beginning, which was rubbish and probably way over the line. With all the drug references, imagine mom buying the album with a huge pill on the cover. The joke of it all is Eric never smoked a joint in his life! It was just naïve, we were trying too hard to be cool."

Jake Duncan felt that a lot of the group's problems stemmed from the fact that no one had taken over as the band's manager since Tam Paton had been fired. "September of 1979, we were in L.A. living in a band house, and I asked Eric casually what we were gonna do manager-wise. He was never comfortable with the idea of someone else calling the shots. I said, 'I know this guy, just a name, but this band needs [to be] managed. Somebody has to look over all this.' And so he called Andy."

Andy Trueman was an industry vet who had worked with Blue Oyster Cult, Ted Nugent, Jethro Tull, and E.L.O. It was an impressive resume, and it got him the gig. Trueman recalled, "My first impression of them is that they were very serious about reinventing their image—and that they had been totally abused by their previous manager. Not physically, but mentally and emotionally. I think Tam found himself in a glamorous position and didn't give a damn about the Bay City Rollers as people. He was out to hustle them and make money for himself. He was no manager. He was a potato salesman and nothing more. Duncan Faure was the new lead singer, and he was very different from Les in that he wasn't a typical stand-up singer. He could play a lot of different instruments. He was real shy when he joined the Rollers, and it took him quite a while to adapt to the role of front man. The biggest thing that Duncan had going for him was his versatility, especially compared to Les McKeown. He was definitely the right guy for the direction that the band wanted to take musically. My first experience with them was a twenty-five-date U.S. tour in September of '79. It was the *Elevator* tour with Todd Rundgren's Utopia, which ultimately had to be shortened because of poor ticket sales." Contributing factors included lack of promotion for *Elevator* and the financial constraints brought on by the gas crisis that had Americans paying more than a dollar for a gallon of gas for the first time ever.

With the free time afforded by the cancellations, Trueman went to work on another plan. "I spent most of the time after the U.S. tour on the phone, making calls to England. I figured that is where we should concentrate on working the record. Meanwhile, Duncan went home to South Africa to see what he could do about getting some response there. I should add that at this time Arista had already given up on the band and offered no assistance at all. With Duncan's help, we were able to work a deal in South Africa for the release of a single on EMI. I devised a publicity campaign, and in three weeks time 'Hello and Welcome Home' was a top-ten hit there, and that's when it all turned sour. The South African press is the absolute worst in the world. They will go out of their way to cause trouble in print to sell papers. I sensed from the beginning that we were primed for a set up. The night of our first gig in South Africa, Duncan says on stage, 'It's great to be back in South Africa ... fuckin' great.' Next day, every bloody paper had us in the headlines: 'Four-Letter Faure' they called him. And that was just the beginning. We had gone to great lengths to design a show with outstanding pyrotechnics that were as good, if not better, than what KISS were using at the time. We had permits, a licensed operator—it didn't matter. In both Durban and Johannesburg we were ordered by the fire marshall not to use them. As a result, we were forced to cancel other indoor shows. Attendance dropped, and I made a business decision to cancel the tour after I'd spent over $37,000 of my own money."

Toasting the 'engagement' of Tam Paton and Marcella Knaiflova, 1976. CREDIT: Tam Paton Collection

There's a Roller in my tree, 1976.

Pat McGlynn

In NYC with Pat McGlynn still in good graces. CREDIT: Bob Gruen/Starfile

Down to a foursome in 1977

Eric Faulkner

Les McKeown

Stuart 'Woody' Wood

Derek Longmuir

At New York's famous 'Studio 54' with club owner Steve Rubell.

Elevator promo pic, 1979, CREDIT: Arista Records Publicity

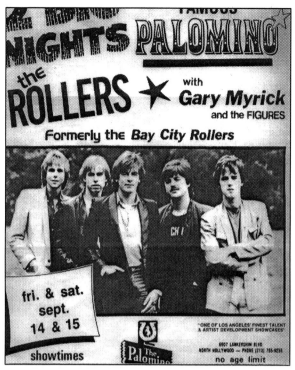

Getting the word out. The boys are back in L.A.

Duncan, Derek, and Eric chill backstage, 1980.

Advertisement for the ill fated 1980 South African tour.

Somber at sound check in South Africa. CREDIT:
Ruphin Coudyzer/ *The Star*

The 'Life On The Radio' video featured the Rollers as 1920s era crooners. CREDIT: CBS Publicity

The Band at the Peppermint Lounge. New York, 1981. CREDIT: Bob Gruen / Starfile

Japan, 1982 and the gang's all here (except Duncan).

As close as they'd ever be, Les and Eric.

Welcome to the '90s. Duncan Faure,
still tartan after all these years. 1990.
CREDIT: Duncan Faure

After bumping into each other at an L.A. supermarket, Ian and
Duncan, who had never played together before, form "The
Joybuzzers." Shown here on stage in San Jose. CREDIT:
Duncan Faure

Publicity shot for the 1993 Edition of the BCR. CREDIT: Jeff Hubbard Productions.

1993 U.S. Tour (L-R) Eric, Kass, Woody, Alan. CREDIT: Jeff Hubbard Productions

Duncan Faure and Ian Mitchell, Playing together again
with 'The BlueBottles' hangin' in Hollywood, 1999.
CREDIT: Wayne Coy

Rollers meet radio. Ian and Les with longtime
Radio One star, Tony Blackburn. 1993
CREDIT: Andy Scott / Ian Mitchell.

Les McKeown faces the music, outside the courtroom after being charged with driving while intoxicated in 2003.

Tam Paton, leaving high court, 2002.

Derek Longmuir, outside the courtroom, 1999.

THIRTEEN

Busted and Broke Up

While on tour in South Africa, Andy Trueman was approached by film producer Barry St. Clair. He wanted the Rollers to return in February to appear in his movie, *Burning Rubber*, the story of a racecar driver. On the table was an offer for Alan Longmuir to co-star with Olivia Pascal as his mechanic/love interest. Alan, who had been disappointed when the band had to pass on an offer to appear in the 1977 film *Rollercoaster*, had gotten bit by the acting bug hard while taping the Krofft series. He was keen, so Trueman agreed. There would be parts available for other band members as well. In addition, St. Clair offered the opportunity for the Rollers to provide music for the film's soundtrack. Filming on *Burning Rubber* began on Feb 25 in Tarlton, forty-five minutes north of Johannesburg. Duncan, Woody, and Derek made the trip with Alan. Eric had prior commitments, so he did not appear in the film, but he did supply a song, "New Beginnings," for the soundtrack.

Two weeks after principal photography for the film began, on March 14, Faure, Derek Longmuir, and Wood were at a nightclub called "20th Century" in Johannesburg when they got word that the local police were looking for them. The police were investigating charges that the band was responsible for over $12,000 in debts from their South African tour. Jake Duncan got a call from a panicked Wood at the band's hotel. "Woody called and said, 'I've got some stuff. You need to go to my room and Derek's room. It's in a toothpaste tube on top of the toilet.' I rushed to the desk and got keys. I went and got it all and put it in my briefcase. I drove two blocks and chucked it. When I got back, the Police were waiting outside my room. One of the cops said, 'You're gonna swing for this unless you tell me where the band is.' They put me in a car and we headed to the club. I had no choice except to take them there. Derek was upset beyond belief. He screamed at me, *What the fuck did you tell them for?'* They took our passports and locked us up for two or three nights. A London lawyer called John Tsalacoucas put up the bail money with the agreement that bail equaled returned passports for the band. So they struck a deal and took the next flight out. I had to stay there. The police told me, 'We know you're getting framed for this.' It was totally wrong for them to do that to me. When I got back home, I took them to the U.K. Industrial Tribunal for unfair dismissal and won. Derek showed up and didn't refute any of the allegations about drugs. I looked him in the eye and told him, 'I'm gonna work as hard against you as I ever did for you.' I was raging. I had lost my job over their mistake. Andy Trueman was great through the whole thing, he backed me up and gave me the best advice I've ever received when he said, 'In the future, always stay two steps ahead and two drinks behind.' Those were words of wisdom that I will never forget."

When asked for his account of the legal troubles, Trueman said, "I really have no comment. But I will tell you this: it was because of Derek Longmuir and his stupid attitude about money. It was all prefabricated, and Jake ended up staying in jail when it should have been Derek. I considered a lawsuit later, but I'm the type of person who doesn't want to spend his life looking back." His criticism of the drummer didn't stop there. "It's my opinion that Derek and his paranoia were the downfall of the band. He fancied himself a lawyer or accountant and was always looking over his shoulder to see who might be trying to screw him next. Truth is, he didn't know half as much as he claimed to. His attitude was the reason the Rollers went down the toilet in America. He was a stereotypical Scotsman."

Once again without management and still wounded by the South African fiasco and lack of success with *Elevator*, the band became very defensive in its dealings with Arista Records in 1980. They felt that the label had dropped the ball and failed to support a very good record. Privately, Clive Davis shared his opinion that, without fan favorite McKeown and outside songwriters, the band had no chance of regaining any commercial momentum. The band still owed the label one more release, and in was in no mood to go through another *Elevator* experience with Arista.

"We just slammed together some odds and ends to get out of our deal," says Faure. "It was a maddening time because Eric and Woody just didn't want to bust their asses for nothing again." The Rollers' final Arista release, *Voxx*, was an uneven effort, at best. Comprised of leftovers from the *Elevator* sessions, two Faure songs from the Rabbitt days, and odd inclusions like the traditional Scottish instrumental "The Jig" featuring Faulkner on electric violin. The album also included a live 1977 version of "Rebel Rebel" that had been recorded on tour, in Japan. This ended up being the only country where the album was released. To add to the already depressing series of events, 1980 ended with the assassination of John Lennon in New York on December 8. Beth Wernick, who ran publicist Bob Levinson's New York office, remembers. "The band was in the studio doing some remixing on their album around 11 p.m. and Duncan called me upset, crying with the news of Lennon's death. He wasn't just upset that John had been shot, he was really worried that some crazy person was on the loose shooting people in New York. About two o'clock in the morning, he and Woody showed up at my door and wanted me to go with them to The Dakota. We drove over there in their rental car and stayed outside all night and throughout the next morning. When we finally went to leave on the ninth, the rental car had been towed. Fit ending for an already miserable day."

The parting with Arista was not amicable, as the relationship ended with a frustrated Wood venting his anger toward Clive Davis. Duncan Faure remembers, "Woody told Clive to fuck off. He's probably the only musician to ever tell Clive to fuck off. And then he shelved us. I remember saying to Woods, 'Not a good thing to tell the president of your record company to get stuffed, do ya think?' But hey, that's rock and roll."

With the Arista contract fulfilled and Andy Trueman gone, once again, they were in need of management and turned to Beth Wernick to help them out. "Eric called and asked if we could set up meetings for the band with some of the major New York based artist managers for them. So, I literally called all of them. The one that stood out was Bill Auicoin, who managed KISS. He was such a gentleman. The guys performed some of their new material live in his office at a white baby grand and after it was over, he pulled Duncan and I aside and said 'I think you've got something, a real future, and I'd be interested in talking with you. As far as the Bay City Rollers, I think they're done, but we should talk some more.' Well, Duncan thought about it and politely declined. It was sheer loyalty to the guys. He felt he owed it to them to stick it out. That's just the way he was."

The band ended up enlisting the services of Al Dellentash and David Sonnenburg who co-managed Meatloaf and Southside Johnny. Task one was to negotiate the group's first non Bell/Arista deal. They got what they were looking for at CBS International/Epic where a one album agreement was offered up and quickly agreed to. The band then found new digs for their new project.

They moved into a home in Maplewood, New Jersey, and began work on *Ricochet* at producer Stefan Galfas's "House of Music" studios. "I knew David [Sonnenberg] from Meat Loaf and Al [Dellentash] from the Southside Johnny stuff. They met with me and wanted to know my vision and to see if it matched theirs and the band's. I said I did not want to make a retro-sounding Bay City Rollers album, and they loved that. The band especially was enjoying that we were going to take our time and experiment musically. They wanted a challenge and to push the limits while staying true to their past. As musicians they were good. Damn good. Not extraordinary, but they had a cohesive thing, a vibe that is very rare. Together, they were magic. I remember seeing them play 'Saturday Night' at a gig and thinking that they just had 'it.' In fact, they're one of the last acts that I can say that about.

"*Ricochet* was a tough record to make. The band was at a crossroads creatively, and anytime you go in struggling to figure out what you want the end product to be you can have problems. Alcohol definitely played a part. Not while they were working, but it was in the air. Also they had endured so much criticism. They're gay or they don't play on the records, all of that adds to a bit of tension, or a better word would be insecurity. Truth is, the experience was pleasant, and there was no friction. The only trauma was their own inner demons. Tam had put them through their paces at a young age, and they would want to talk about it and I'd say look guys, I'm not your therapist, I'm not your friend, I'm here to do one thing and that is to make a damn good record with you. I said the past was a drag, I know, but let's forget the past and move forward."

Armed with a new batch of songs written by Faure and Faulkner, the Rollers went about their recording at a pace they had never enjoyed before. They would record during the day and return to the house afterwards. Faure remembers, "I had written an instrumental called 'Ricochet' for one of my brother's films, which worked out nicely. And of course, 'Doors, Bars, and Metal' was about our time in jail. Eric's 'Life on the Radio' was great. All in all, a pretty good bunch of songs to choose from."

Producer Galfas was impressed with their writing. "From a songwriting standpoint, they were really searching for an identity. Six or seven of the songs really stand out. 'Ride' was fun but I thought an odd choice for a single. 'Doors, Bars, and Metal' had a very interesting feel and some cool vocal things going on. 'Life on the Radio' brought that whole Scottish thing with the bagpipe break, and 'Ricochet' was cool because it started as an instrumental and stayed that way. With a group so known for its vocals, to not only record and keep it on the album but to actually name the record *Ricochet* was pretty bold. 'Won't You Come Home With Me' was gorgeous and could be a hit if it was released today. But my favorite track didn't make it on the album for some reason. It's called 'Statue of Liberty.' Just too deep, I guess, to include it. But man, it was a real statement. Very prophetic, especially in the wake of 9/11. It kind of gets into the jealousy that those who are not born here in the States feel. Amazing."

The sessions were also noteworthy for the lack of tension that had come to be expected at Rollers recording dates. In fact, says Galfas, it could get down right giddy at times. "The day that management brings all of the head honchos from the label to the studio to hear how it's going just happens to be the day that Eric Faulkner decides to come to work dressed completely as a woman. His creative juices were really flowing and he's at the studio in full-on fishnet stockings, garter belt, mini-skirt, heels, and makeup. He looked great. The record company people didn't know what to think, Al and David didn't know what to think. We laughed our asses off after they left." Another anecdote from their time in New Jersey comes courtesy of Beth Wernick, who was living in the Maplewood house with the group. And it also involved Faulkner. "I usually got up earlier than the band because I wasn't up late partying as much they were. I walk into the kitchen on a Sunday morning and there were two girls at the table, black hair dye, black fingernails, kinda punk looking. I said, 'Hello…and who are you?' They explained that they were in from Manhattan and that Eric had them brought over by cab the night before. My first thought was 'that had to be expensive,' and my second was 'Eric! They have to get up and go. We had to get to the studio.' So, we got them homeward bound and Eric was running around in his underwear that said 'Rollers' and two dice on the crotch area, fuming that the girls had put something in his drink or drugged him somehow. The band is ready to go to work but Eric refuses to get dressed. He insists that we go to the studio and that he wouldn't be wearing any additional clothes. All the way there, he continued to moan about how he had been slipped a mickey by those punk girls. After we got to the studio, Derek pulled me aside and said 'please get him some clothes.' So, I headed out to find some. Sunday morning in Jersey, not a lot open. So I ended up grabbing some sweats at a local swap meet and took them back. He had come down from whatever he was on by that time and begrudgingly got dressed, much to everyone's relief." Compared to the stressful year that preceded it, it was now a laugh a minute at "Roller Central."

Also contributing to the levity was the unspoken but always prevalent opinion that if *Ricochet* failed to break through, it was more than likely going to be their final album. In a way, it was a 'what have we got to lose attitude' that alleviated any pressure. It also didn't hurt that, unlike previous projects, this was a low-budget affair, more about the work than living the 'rock stars making an album' vibe. Says Galfas, "We were very budget conscious. I worked for half of what I usually get up front. The band stayed in a rented house. In the end, we made a $250,000 record for $100,000, which is unheard of. The band was driven to make a great record, and it was my studio so I wouldn't let them stop until we got it right. Cheap Trick, who were also on Epic, was supposed to come and guest on a song or two, but somehow it never happened. I'm glad it didn't because I don't think we needed that whole guest star thing. These guys were looking to make a statement of their own, and they did."

He remembers the Rollers as a unit, but also as five unique individuals. "Eric was out of his mind in a wonderful way. His thick Scots accent. He could have fired me twenty times and I would have never known 'cause I couldn't understand half of what he said. The only Gaelic saying I know I learned from him: 'Yen Mare,' which means, 'one more.' He was constantly saying that whenever he'd want another crack at a solo. He had a great vibe, a positive energy. He drank like a fish, but never while we were working.

"Woody was a genius. So underrated and unsung as a player. Very intuitive musically and so willing to push the limits in the studio. Idea after idea. Duncan wanted to be John Lennon and the Rollers to be the Beatles. They were such an influence on him that we had to work hard to get past that. I'd remind him that it was okay for Rabbitt, but I needed him to be true to himself. Beyond that little issue, he has an amazing voice; he's an awesome guitarist and great on the keyboards, which was a new element for the band. He was starting to lose his hair in the back and was very concerned about that, and he was manic. His energy was incredible, and he would literally work twelve hours a day if that's what it took to get it right. Derek was a bit on the conservative side compared to the rest. He had invented a style of drumming with the Bay City Rollers that was cool and corny. He was a thumper. Great timekeeper, but afraid to swing. That was a real challenge. But listen to the album, we got him to swing, and he's a very good drummer. Alan was there and *looked* great. Seriously, he was the one who kind of stayed in the background. A lot of vocal takes, harmonies. He didn't play as much as the others on the record, but trust me, the local bars knew him well."

The marketing department at Epic was floored when they heard the final product. As with *Elevator*, the band had delivered a good—no, a very good—record. And like their predecessors at Arista, they had no idea what to do with it. Promotion man Barry Lyons and his team came up with a plan. They would release the album in Canada only to start, followed by Great Britian, Germany, and Japan. If it worked, the rest of the world would follow. It would be packaged in a plain brown paper wrapper with the words "CONTAINS ONE GREAT ROCK ALBUM" on the front. No pictures, not a mention of the band's name. Songwriting credits went to "Tom, Dick, Harry, and Sam." If they could get a buzz at retail or radio that way, they would reveal who was behind it all after opinions had been formed. The first part of the equation worked. The 'plain wrapper' version sold more than expected, and radio even played a few of the tracks including "Ride" and "Life on the Radio." With videos for both songs plus "Doors, Bars, and Metal" in the can, they held their breath as it was announced that the purveyors of these new exciting sounds were indeed the Rollers.

The Canadian reaction was immediate after the album was released with its regular sleeve. Airplay and in-store spins disappeared overnight. New cable network MTV rescinded on their promise to rotate the videos, and it was over almost as soon as it began. The public had spoken, loud and clear. The negative image of the band was so strong that they would not be able to get past it—no matter how good the music was.

Stefan Galfas has this theory: "It was released in a brown paper bag. Doesn't that say it all? The label and their managers had this self-fulfilling prophecy of failure. If you tell yourself something enough it'll come true. The decision to use 'the Rollers' instead of 'the Bay City Rollers' was ill conceived. I mean, we're talking about a brand name here. They were not giving the public any credit and forgetting that people aren't as sophisticated as you think. Tell them who it is! They were starting from scratch and not using any of the equity that the name brought to the table. So now you're breaking a brand new band. Why? If they would have toured for a year and come back in to the studio with me, I guarantee you we would have made one hell of a follow-up record. It would have blown you away ... gone! But the label decided to cut their losses in the end, and that was it for the Bay City Rollers."

A few gigs followed the crash-and-burn *Ricochet* release. This time around there were no stadiums, arenas, or festivals. The band had to settle for small clubs like Malibu in Long Island, Beggar's Opera in Queens, the Whisky in Los Angeles, and even Harrah's Casino in Lake Tahoe. By the end of 1981, the group decided to call it a day. It was evident that continuing was not in anyone's best interests. For Duncan Faure it was a trip home to South Africa at Christmas that convinced him. "I brought *Ricochet* back and made the rounds with my radio friends. No one would play it. I kept hearing Rabbitt and even this silly Christmas song that I had recorded. And that was a pretty loud message: 'We'll play your stuff, but we're not interested in the Rollers at all.' I got it right then, and it still hurts to think about. My feelings on the Rollers are that I loved them and would have them back in a second. I believe the world missed out because of a lot of small-minded idiots who had a mental block against our band. Pity. Cause we were damn good. As good as they come."

FOURTEEN

L.A. Girls

No book on a pop phenomenon like the Bay City Rollers would be complete without a look into the mindset of their most devoted fans, three of whom told their story for this project. Like Caroline Sullivan—who chronicled her obsession in the book *Bye Bye Baby, My Tragic Love Affair With the Bay City Rollers*—these three women, all in their forties now, got the opportunity to get close to the group in the late 1970s in Los Angeles. Their common thread is their need to know the band members as intimately as possible, and that in every single instance that conquest carried an emotional price.

GAIL

"It was 1976, and I was attending junior high in Torrance. I skipped school to go see them at Wherehouse Records. Most kids didn't like them. It was just a small group of girls. Pictures in our lockers, we dressed like them and bought all of the magazines. We spent every available cent on Roller-related stuff. I couldn't drive, so my parents had to take me every time there was a TV taping or radio appearance. We did them all, Don Kirshner's *Rock Concert*, *Mike Douglas*, *Merv Griffin*, *Bill Cosby*, all of them. There were probably fifteen to twenty regulars that you would see at all of the shows. It got very competitive amongst us with everyone trying to be first to know what time sound check would be or what hotel they were staying in. My mom was great through it all, racing to be first in line or whatever.

"By '78 or so, I was very good at the game, and my mom got me a present for my birthday: a room at the LeParc Hotel, which is where all of the guys except Les were staying while they taped the Krofft show. I was only fourteen but looked eighteen or twenty. I took it one step further by erasing the 'four' in my birth year [1964] on my ID card and changing it to a 'one.' So, for all intents and purposes, I was eighteen. And you can probably guess what those intents were. It didn't take long; I bumped into them the first day, and we started to talk.

"Eric came to me and said that I needed to keep it all low-key. He warned me to stay away from the other fans, which, of course, made them not like me very much. We'd go to their rooms, usually just two or three of us girls. Of course, I thought I was special. Turns out, they all thought that. I slept with Eric a few times in those two months.

"When Duncan joined and Les was out, they would come back to California quite often. There was a bit of competition then. Duncan told me that Eric was not my type and that he, of course, was. I listened and started spending most of my time with him. I wasn't his girlfriend yet, but he would call me as soon as they landed in L.A. The others would take a limo to their hotel; Duncan and I would go in my car and check into our own room elsewhere. That went on for a few years. Eventually, we moved into an apartment on Sunset together. He had broken up with his girlfriend, Francine, and about a year later we bought a house together in Granada Hills. It gave Duncan more space, and he and Woods a place to stay in L.A. while they worked on their post-Rollers stuff.

"It was great for a while … I was working my butt off. The guys weren't getting any money from their music, so we added roommates, a girl named Rebecca, a friend of mine from school named Michelle, Russell Issamon from New Jersey, and Laurie McClain. It was a complete madhouse! We had seven people living there and countless others coming and going. It was constant fighting and way too much partying. I ended up breaking up with Duncan after he cheated on me. He had always flirted, but never cheated. One day, I came home and Woody said, 'Don't go upstairs, you'll get hurt.' Of course I did, and *I did*. He would say, 'Oh, it's just sex, I don't have feelings for them like I do you.' At first I tried to be cool, thinking it was only a phase. I thought it would get better, but it only got worse … orgies and everything. Duncan wanted me to sleep with him and other girls at the same time. It really messed with my head. Then, he found out I lied about my age and totally freaked, screaming at me. I was confused and scared.

Woody had always been there to comfort me, help with the laundry whatever. When Duncan lost it with me, I went to him, and that night my BCR sex scoreboard went up by one. Three Rollers—which isn't even a record. I think Diane had four! The time after that was rough. We were desperate to keep the house, so I made a few adult films to pay the bills. Not proud of it, but something had to be done. By 1984, I'd had enough. I met a guy at a taping of the TV show *Solid Gold*. We hit it off, and I put the whole Roller thing and everything that went with it behind me. We moved to North Carolina and that's where I am still today. I'd be lying if I said I don't look back and wonder what might have happened if I'd stayed. Duncan eventually married Laurie; Woody's married too. I have tried to reach out to them, but they really don't have much to say. In fact, Woody's wife made it very clear that I needed to stay away. That's cool. It's all a part of growing up, I guess."

DIANE

"In 1974, I spent the summer with my grandmother in England. I saw the Rollers on the *Shang A Lang* show every day. All the British girls were crazy for them, most were still in school. Musically, it was like a step up from the Partridge Family and the Monkees, plus they had all that tartan, and it was very exciting. Grandma would go to Woolworth's and buy the 45s for me, so by the time I went home I had quite the collection. Obviously, I was way ahead of the U.S. in knowing who they were and everything. Not long after, I got yanked out of regular school and put into an all-girls Catholic school. You had to put something up in your locker, so it was the Bay City Rollers for me. So cutting edge!

"It was quite a big deal when they were on the *Howard Cosell Show*. I remember thinking, 'Finally, they'll get some recognition.' Eric and Les were my favorites; we went to greet them on their first visit to the West Coast. After that, it was a big blur of being yelled at and kicked out of TV tapings because we were too young. The Krofft show was the best, we'd take turns spending the night to get tickets and save a place in line for each other. It was weird because we had moved on to the Sex Pistols and the Clash musically, but still had a thing for the guys. We had to drink Bacardi and Coke or smoke pot just to get through it. I really felt sorry for them having to endure Eric Estrada, H.R. Puffenstuff, and Sha Na Na! You could tell they hated it too. It made them all very terse and nasty. I remember trying to engage Les in a conversation about music and we got to the subject of the female band the Runaways [Joan Jett, Lita Ford] and he just gave me this look of disgust and said, 'They're nothing but a bunch of talentless dykes.' Eric wasn't any better. Drinking all the time, just drunk and bitter. They could see the end was near. We knew cause Les had told us he was leaving.

"In the Summer of '79, we were all at Le Parc. I remember it was all Eagles and Blondie and lots of drinking and drugs. Eric would invite me to his room for the white wine and marijuana combo. He drank, I smoked, and he would play me tapes of his new songs. The other girls would get jealous and say, 'He's only into you cause you're into the music.' Which I was. They just wanted him to be 'in to' them in other ways.

"Duncan was very nice but a big perv. His big thing was to get two girls at the same time. Still is, I hear. Les was always all over me too, especially when I worked at Baskin Robbins Ice Cream … very convenient for a rock star with the munchies. He was the one for me. Looking back, I can thank him for getting me into bands. I still talk to him but now—it's different. It's regular stuff, George Bush, travel, and of course my therapy bills, which are all his fault."

KIM

"I was twelve years old when I fell in love with the Rollers on the Ann-Margret TV special. They were so different! The clothes, the accents. Up until then, I kind of preferred Bowie and The Who but, then I saw Eric and thought, 'He's the most gorgeous thing I've ever laid eyes on.' I wanted to marry him and have twenty kids.

"We did all the TV shows, *Mike Douglas*, *Midnight Special*, *Dinah Shore*, *Bandstand*. The coolest was *Merv Griffin*—he actually went outside and got us and let us sit on the stage even though we were too young. My mom was doing the best she could as a single parent, but looking back, I think I rebelled against her and her boyfriends that weren't my dad. The Rollers were a good source for venting that rebellion.

"By 1978, it had all gotten very sad. We would sit outside of the house on Laurel Canyon just hoping to see them. I sat outside that house for four months while 'the Hillside Strangler' was killing people all around me. Literally risking our lives for the Bay City Rollers! I remember Eric being dropped off by a cab, drunk, and having to pay his fare with quarters. I needed to make a call, so he gave me one too. I'll never forget the smell of his 'Paco Rabann' cologne and vodka—or whatever he'd been drinking—together. He was the first one I got close to, and he was very sweet. Kind of like a father figure. It was really weird.

"In '79, things came to a head between my mom and me. I grabbed all my clothes and put them on the roof. I found out that the Rollers were at Le Parc, so that was where I headed. I ended up moving in with these guys from Scotland who had a place just across the street from the hotel. I soon found out that Eric, Woody, and Duncan were basically male whores, getting it wherever they could. In the pool, in the sauna—my sister and Duncan actually did it in the bed next to me. I wrapped up the summer with Les at the 'Magic Hotel.' And, it was, by the way.

"Then, I didn't see them 'till '81 at the Roxy, and they were all really rude to me. I just thought, 'Oh things aren't going well for them, maybe they'll be nicer next time.' Sadly, there never was a next time. Now, I spend a lot of time on the Internet, buying back my teenage memories and Bay City Rollers memorabilia. A lot of it is stuff I threw away when I outgrew them. When you think about it, I guess I never really did."

EPILOGUE

Game, Set, Match

The Bay City Rollers story did not end in 1981. The years that have passed since have featured many headlines and reunions. Indiana-based talent agent Jeff Hubbard first became involved with the band in 1988. "I met Eric just outside of Toronto. I was there doing some work with Gary Lewis and the Playboys. Bill Geffros was the house agent for 'Lulu's Roadhouse,' which is in the *Guinness Book* for having the world's longest bar. Anyway, Bill told me he had the Bay City Rollers booked, and of course I had to go and check it out. Anyone who was a teenager in 1975 knew who they were. Anyway, Bill introduced me to Eric and his girlfriend, Kass. As it turns out, we were staying at the same hotel. I invited them to go fishing with me, and we had a great time. Eric loves to fish. I told him I was a booking agent and that I might be able to get them some work. He gave me his number and said call me if you get anything happening. I did, and that's how that first tour came about. We ended up doing a two or three-week run. Eric was the only original in the band at that time."

They would reconvene in 1993 with a couple of other familiar faces. "Eric informed me that he had Woody and Al back in the band and that he was hoping to get Derek as well. We booked three weeks worth of dates in '93. They were very easy to work with as a whole, but touring is always hard work and it can get the best of anyone, so I'd be lying if I said it was all wonderful. There were moments, like there are on any tour. We traveled a long way by van and car, so it was a long three weeks. Three weeks of listening to Eric practice his guitar playing. The shows went over pretty well, selling about sixty to eighty percent of capacity everywhere. The biggest drag was the audience's total disregard for the new songs. They just wanted the hits and would literally walk out during the new stuff. It probably didn't help that Eric was the singer. He's the most underrated guitarist in the world, I mean Eddie Van Halen *wishes* he could play like Eric, but singing isn't what he does best, and it showed. We thought a lot about how much Les would add, but then you'd have to deal with him as a human being. The guy is a complete asshole, so we didn't go there. All in all, we were happy with the tour."

Besides touring, the group has been the subject of quite a few television documentaries. Hubbard remembers one in particular: "I got a call in 1996. A guy named 'Tak' from Japan. He and his partner 'Tino' wanted to do a documentary on the Rollers. Somehow, he had gotten my number. I called Eric. He said sure and then he got Les and Ian to agree to do it too. I think they flew to L.A. to interview Ian at his home and did the Les and Eric stuff in the U.K."

The BBC and VH1 specials that ran in 1999 found the group looking closer than ever to being truly reunited. As the new millenium dawned, the Longmuirs, Faulkner, McKeown, and Wood were all on board along with a new manager Mark St. John.

Unity was the prevailing message in an *Edinburgh Evening News* article on the band, in which Les McKeown said, "There was a time when Eric and I couldn't stand being in the same country as each other, never mind the same room."

Faulkner agreed, saying, "It's been great working together again, and the reunion has been surprisingly painless." Both mentioned the money due the band as incentive to bury the hatchet. "People think we got paid millions when Rollermania was at it's peak, but we didn't. That's why we had to keep touring, to survive. The bills didn't stop coming in, but the royalties did."

McKeown added, "We reckon we've sold in excess of 120 million records worldwide, but we've never been paid a penny. To say we're pissed off is an understatement."

Stuart Wood remained optimistic in that regard. "Hopefully, we'll get our money back. We worked hard for it so we should get the rewards."

Derek Longmuir told the *Daily Record* that the group's interpersonal issues were definitely on the mend, saying, "We are pals now. We went through a bad time, but we're older and more mature."

The reformed Rollers agreed to bring in the century with a live performance at Edinburgh's New Year's Hogmanay celebration. Shortly after that gig, a deal with U.S. label Bodyguard Records was struck. The plan was to release a live CD from a 1977 Japanese show first and then follow up with a studio album of all-new material. Label head Dr. Gene Foley recalls, "Eric had the master tapes from 1977. The process was like this: we would do a mix, send a CD burn via Fed-Ex to the band. They would listen, suggest a change or two, and send it back. This went on for a while until we had a mix that they all liked and agreed on. Then their manager, Mark St. John, sent over the artwork and liner notes complete and ready to print. We pressed it and released it."

Whether it was the negative publicity surrounding Derek Longmuir's arrest for possession of pornographic materials involving minors or the same old negative image issues, the album did not fare well, and that put the brakes on releasing the studio album. Says Foley, "The decision was made by us all to not do that after the sales of the live CD didn't live up to expectations. I think all together we only sold about 500 copies of that. We scanned 300 or so and sold another 200 online and that's it. Obviously, those numbers are pretty disappointing. We had baby bands that would sell more than that from a box in their trunk at their gigs. It was a business decision to not follow through with the new studio album. It's pretty difficult to get investors interested after those kinds of sales figures. We did have a meeting; John [Rollo] my former partner and others met with Eric, Les, and Woody and their manager in London. The advance they needed was just way too much to take that kind of a risk." So, the holy grail of Rollers collectibles is now gathering dust. "I have a CD with five or six new Bay City Rollers songs from '99—probably in a file back at the old label offices. I can tell you that it was very good. One song, 'Gossamer Dream,' was used at the tail end of the VH1 special, and it's amazing. It obviously needed a little more tweaking, but the songs are very good. All of the new material was written by the band themselves."

Foley is disappointed that it didn't work out. "It's pretty sad that it didn't happen. They had the best manager they've ever had. They had the momentum from the VH1 special and were getting along, for the most part. Obviously they had a great label situation. It just hinged on that live album doing better than it did. The irony of it is that before we released it, I was deluged with emails from the fans saying that they were going to buy it. Some did, but not nearly enough of them."

Or maybe, timing *is* everything. In 2003, a collection of BCR hits went to number 1 in the U.K. "Bye Bye Baby" was featured prominently in the hit film *Love Actually*, and "Saturday Night" was the soundtrack to a succesful Planter's Peanuts television campaign. McKeown's autobiography sold briskly. Jeff Hubbard says the interest is definitely still there. "I still get inquiries about them. In fact, just recently, I sent a letter to Eric to inform him of the latest offer. Three weeks for a couple hundred thousand. I haven't heard back, so he either doesn't need the money or maybe he can't be bothered. I don't know if he even read the letter."

Books and magazine articles continue to be written, and thousands of fans throughout the world keep up with the former members and their activities on the Internet and at fan conventions. It is doubtful that they'll ever get the credit that many believe they deserve for enduring it all—or that they'll make any new music together. Not to mention ever recover any of the money that they claim is owed to them in back royalties by Arista

Records. But one thing is for sure: they will forever be bound as brothers by their time together, pioneers in the world of teen pop. Hubbard recalls one incident moment on the road with the Rollers: "We were traveling from L.A. to Vegas. This big, long stretch of nothing. Woody decides that he needs to piss—and right now. So, we pull the van over in the middle of the Mojave Desert. Woody goes trudging up a hill to take a leak. Next thing you know, Alan's right beside him with his arm around his shoulder. I will never forget that sight of the two Bay City brothers happily pissing in the desert breeze with their arms around each other. I guess the band that urinates together, stays together. Say want you want about them, but they were a lot of fun."

SO ... WHERE ARE THEY NOW?

Tam Paton

Imprisoned in 1982 for indiscretions with minors. A successful property manager. Completely retired from the music business. Has been in and out of trouble with Scottish police over the past few years. First for allegations made by individuals about sexual misconduct in the 1970s (including Pat McGlynn), and then for possession of drugs.

Derek Longmuir

Participated in a couple of Japanese reunion tours. Retired from music to become a registered nurse in Edinburgh. Was found guilty of possession of pornographic materials involving minors and has maintained an extremely low profile since. Took part in the late 90s BBC and VH1 television specials on the band and the 1999 recording sessions. Lives in Scotland.

Alan Longmuir

Continued to record with and appear in various formations of the BCR until suffering a heart attack in 1995 and a stroke in 1997 that left him partially paralyzed. Recently registered a legal partnership with co-director Stuart Wood (Bay City Rollers Ltd.) that includes Faulkner, McKeown, and Derek Longmuir as non voting board members. Twice married (now to Eileen), he has a son (Jordan) from his first marriage and lives in Scotland.

Nobby Clark

Completely left the music business and became one of the U.K.'s premiere experts on the subject of mold and mildew removal. Suffered bouts of depression and alcoholism. After recovering he recorded and released his first album in over thirty years. Married with a daughter and since divorced, he lives in Scotland.

Stuart "Woody" Wood

Recorded and toured with other ex-BCR members over the years. Formed a three-piece band called Karu in the early eighties with Duncan Faure. Also a member of "the Passengers" and "the Bond." Now recording traditional Celtic folk music with an updated feel, including the extremely successful "Scottish Moods." Married (Denise) and living in Scotland.

Eric Faulkner

Tried valiantly to keep the Bay City Rollers alive through the '80s and '90s, touring and recording as "the New Rollers" and then as the Bay City Rollers. Won a successful legal battle with Les McKeown over usage of the name. After producing the debut for new artist "Steadman," he participated in the 2000 reunion effort with the others and then disappeared from public life. Now using the original family spelling "Falconer" for his surname, he's reportedly still living with his girlfriend (Kass). They have a child and maintain residences in Sussex England, Scotland, and the South of France.

Les McKeown

One of the most active former Rollers. Enjoyed success as a solo artist in Germany and Japan. Participated in recording and concert reunions over the years. Had a very public quarrel with Faulkner that culminated in a legal battle over the rights to use the band's name. A judge ruled that he could continue to perform using it as long as he attached some historical reference to the billing. Has been fronting Les McKeown's '70s" or "Legendary" Bay City Rollers ever since. Authored the only autobiography by a former member, *Shang A Lang: Life As An International Pop Idol*. Married (Keiko) with a child (son Jube, aka Rikki), he lives in London. Has recently turned his anger away from Faulkner and toward Tam Paton. He is very public about his dislike for the former BCR manager, and even confronted him on camera in a 2004 British documentary titled *Who Got the Rollers Millions?* which opened with the singer driving alone to Paton's home for their face-to-face meeting, repeatedly rehearsing his demand, "Give me my money. Where's my fucking money?" It is a mantra he continues to this day.

Ian Mitchell

Continued his musical career after the Rollers as a solo artist and as a member of numerous bands including "Rosetta Stone," the "Ian Mitchell Band," "Bachelor of Hearts," "La Rox," and "The JoyBuzzers" with Duncan Faure. Still remains very popular, especially in Japan and the U.S. Spent some time as a motivational speaker. Is now married (Wendy-Ann Antanaitis) and is a U.S. citizen living in Orange County. He continues to tour and play the BCR hits with his own band.

Pat McGlynn

Enjoyed immediate success in Japan after being fired by the Bay City Rollers. Has participated in numerous reunion concerts and recordings. Went to the Scottish newspapers in 2002 to make his claims of being abused by Tam Paton public. Lives with his wife (Janine Andrews) and daughter Mia in Scotland.

Duncan Faure

Spent the post-Roller '80s and '90s as a solo artist and member of "Karu" with Woody Wood and "The Joybuzzers" with Ian Mitchell. Had one of his songs featured on the Madonna *Who's That Girl* soundtrack in 1987. Has released an album every three years since 1990. Married (Laurie) with two children, he lives in South Africa, and is planning to relocate to the U.S. in 2005.

Andy Trueman-

After being fired by the Rollers, continued to work with rock bands throughout the '80s and '90s. Managed the group "Alcatrazz." And guitarist Yngwie Malmsteen. Died after suffering a massive heart attack in 2002.

The "Fab Five" minus Derek, 1999.

BAY CITY ROLLERS DISCOGRAPHY

Album Title	Year	Label/Catalog #	Producer(s)
Rollin'	1974	Bell/244	Martin/Coulter
Once Upon A Star	1975	Bell/8001	Wainman
Wouldn't You Like It	1975	Bell/8002	Wainman
Bay City Rollers	1975	Arista/4049	Martin/Coulter/ Wainman
Rock 'N' Roll Love Letter	1976	Arista/4071	Wainman
Dedication	1976	Arista/4096	Ienner
It's a Game	1977	Arista/7004	Maslin
Greatest Hits	1977	Arista/4158	Various
Strangers in the Wind	1978	Arista/4194	Maslin
Elevator	1979	Arista/4241	Ker
Voxx	1980	Arista/202204	Ker/Fender
Ricochet	1981	Epic/85004	Galfas

Album Title	Year Label/Catalog #	Producer(s)
Live in Japan	1982 Teichiku/67576V	Bay City Rollers
Breakout	1985 London/L28P1218	Bay City Rollers
Breakout '85	1985 Powderworks/6015	Bay City Rollers
Burning Rubber Soundtrack	1986 Fan Club Cassette	Faulkner/Faure
Rollerworld Live @ Budokan	1999 Bodyguard	Faulkner

ACKNOWLEDGEMENTS

The author wishes to thank the following for their cooperation and valuable assistance in this project:

Andy Trueman, Barry Fasman, Beth Wernick, Big Jim Sullivan, Bill Martin, Bob Gruen, Bob Levinson, Carole Strauss-Klenfner, Chris Spedding, Clive Davis, Colin Frechter, Danny Fields, Dave Eager, Dave Sholin, David Stein, Dee Dee Kirkpatrick, Dick Leahy, Duncan Faure, Emperor Rosko, Dr. Gene Foley, Gerd Beusken, Gin DeMola, Gigi Houghton, Hannes Jonnson, Harry Maslin, Hedy End, Ian Mitchell, Jake Duncan, Jeff Hubbard, Jimmy Ienner, Jonathan King, Ken Sharp, Laurie Faure, Lori Sellstrom, Mike Klenfner, Mike Mansfield, Muff Winwood, Nobby Clark, Pat McGlynn, Peter Stern, Phil Wainman, Rick Cooper, Roger Ashby, Ron Alexenburg, Sid Bernstein, Stefan Galfas, Stuart Wood, Tam Paton, The L.A. Girls, Wendy Antanaitis.

BIBLIOGRAPHY

The Bay City Rollers by Tam Paton with Michael Wale, *Shang A Lang* by Les McKeown, *The London Evening Standard*, Arista Records Publicity, *Edinburgh Daily News, Music Maker, Superpop, Edinburgh Evening News, New York Daily News, Toronto Sun, Billboard Magazine*, BBC Television, *Scottish Daily Record & Sunday Mail, U.S. World News, Starmakers and Svengalis* by Johnny Rogan, *New Musical Express, Record Mirror, '16'* magazine, *Bay City Rollers Magazine, Bye Bye Baby* by Caroline Sullivan, *Teen Stars Today, Power Pop* by Ken Sharp, *It's Sid Bernstein Calling* by Sid Bernstein, "The Bay City Rollers Discography" by Hannes Jonnson, *Bay City Rollers* by Ellis Allen, *People Weekly, New York Times, Rolling Stone, The Toronto Star*, VH1 Television, *Creem, Hit Parader, Parade, Story Of Pop, Rock Show, Seventeen, Tiger Beat, Teen Beat, Uncut, Trouser Press, Melody Maker, Eye To Eye, Daily Mail*, CBS Records Publicity, *The All Music Book Of Hit Singles, Who's Your Fave Rave?* by Danny Fields and Randi Reisfeld.

"Money Honey" by Faulkner/Wood. Lyrics reprinted with kind permission of Complete Music Publishing.

ABOUT THE AUTHOR

For the past quarter century, Wayne Coy has made his living a multiple-award-winning radio program director and morning show host. Before *Bay City Babylon*, his previous writing experience included freelance work for newspapers and magazines in Northern California. He also spent time as the top forty radio editor for *GAVIN*, the highly respected San Francisco-based weekly music trade publication.

Coy is married with four children and resides in central Virginia.